Contents

Acknowledgments

Three friends—Sally Keating, Dee Jenkins, and Jack Woods—goaded me into investigating the possibility of writing the biography of Irene Webster-Smith, whom I had met casually just once many years before, but had known of through others in Inter-Varsity Christian Fellowship and World Vision. When Sensei herself visited our home in Merion in August, 1964, I became genuinely convinced that this was a life story well worth recording. Later in the fall I traveled about Japan with her as my expert and tireless guide. Returning by way of Europe, I stopped off in England long enough to visit Adelaide Soal, then rushed home to complete the book by a spring deadline.

It is impossible to list the number of friends who gave valuable help in compiling the story, but I am especially grateful to my wife Lillian who transcribed reams of tape-recorded material and several drafts of the typescript. Most important was her prayerful aid as we lived the book for many months.

Finally I am thankful for Carli Laklan, who perked up my dull prose, as we both worked under the direction of Edward R. Sammis, consulting editor of Harper & Row.

RUSSELL T. HITT

Merion Station, Pennsylvania
September, 1965

SENSEI

I

Mountain into the Sea

Japan's Inland Sea, dotted with islands and surrounded by rocky palisades and rolling hills that reach toward purple mountains, has long been noted for its fabled beauty. The Japanese call the sea *suwo nada,* and its blue waters separate the main island of Honshu from the southern islands of Shikoku and Kyushu.

On the coast of Osaka Bay, the northeast arm of the sea, the great ports of Osaka and Kobe are sheltered, and smaller towns dot the green hills or snuggle peacefully along the shoreline. It was in this pleasant north-shore area that the first inhabitants of Japan settled many centuries ago. It was here that Japanese culture had its birthplace, and here that the earliest capitals were built.

And it was to this same area that British missionaries, led by a stalwart aristocratic Anglican rector named Barclay Buxton, came in the early 1900's. They called themselves the Japan Evangelistic Band, and this quaint name caused many later members to be plagued with such questions as: "What instrument do you play in the band?"

But Buxton's disciples were not a musical band. They were a group bound together by common ideals of biblical holiness, called by God to carry out His work. Only a few came at first, but year by year others followed. The little band grew, and the work went forward.

So it came about that a young Irish woman of good family stood, one beautiful spring morning in the year 1932, on the veranda of Sunrise Home in the city of Akashi, a few miles west of Kobe.

She was Irene Webster-Smith—her family pronounced her name "Irenee." Of medium height, with a huge crown of chestnut colored hair, her round face frequently broke into a smile that turned into a laugh which shook her whole body. Even thick eyeglasses could not conceal her warm and merry expression, and her manner spoke of a talent for combining love with competence.

She stood now drinking in the fresh sea air, surveying the panorama of early dawn loveliness. In the distant east the red sun struggled upward from the waters of the Pacific Ocean. Mists rose from the Inland Sea, gently revealing the tiny islands. Fishermen's boats dotted the bay. Along the coastline smoke spiraled up from hundreds of charcoal fires where fish were drying; in the rice fields, straw-hatted women in their kimonos were already at work.

Irene drew in a long breath. Deep joy flooded through her. How far she had come since that first day when she had felt the call! For a moment she thought back to the months when she had served in the Tokyo Rescue Home that sought to save prostitutes entrapped in the government-licensed brothels. She thought of the shock and grief she had felt when she learned that children were often sold into a life of vice and were trained from earliest years to know no other existence.

And she remembered the thought which had come to her then: *It would be better to put a fence at the top of the precipice than an ambulance at the foot.*

The vision had been born that moment—the vision of a Home, warmed by love and bright with God's grace. A Home where little girls, once destined for brothels, could be brought up in happiness to lead full, useful lives.

In the early sunlight, Irene turned impulsively and looked at Sunrise Home. She saw the long clapboard and stucco building, once a hospital. She saw the broad veranda, the welcoming door. In her mind she saw the twenty-seven little black-haired Japanese girls who would now be chattering over breakfast in the dining room where Miss Mercy Coles, assisted by tiny, sweet-faced Oka-san, presided. But she saw more. She saw her faith child. For Sunrise Home was this.

"Thank you, dear Lord," she murmured. "Thank you."

Then, briskly, she stepped from the veranda and began gathering flowers. She had picked only a few blossoms when the children came pouring from the house. They tumbled over each other in their haste, laughing and calling good morning to their beloved Sensei, which is the Japanese word for "teacher" or "wise one." Everyone, young and old, called Irene *Sensei.*

"O hayo gozai-masu," she laughed. "Good morning! Good morning!"

They surrounded her, eager and bright-eyed. They ranged in

age from three to seventeen, the smallest ones always reminding Irene of dolls.

"We want to help!" Eiko-san cried, hopping up and down in six-year-old excitement. "Let us pick flowers, too!"

"I'll get a vase!" one of the older girls said. "Which room are they for so I'll get just the right one?"

Sensei looked down into the children's faces. "The flowers are not for us today," she said. "They are for our dear Oka-san's little boy, Daishero. I am going to visit him in the hospital in Kobe."

The children became sober. "Is Daishero very ill?" Eiko-san asked.

Sensei nodded, and the children's faces showed quick concern. They all knew the story of Oka-san and little lame Daishero. Not long ago, he and his two older sisters and brother had lived in a small town where his father was the pastor of a small Japanese church. One day, when the older children were at school, Oka-san, with Daishero strapped comfortably to her back, was sitting in the living quarters of their home on the floor above the church, drinking tea with her husband and discussing the hymns which should be sung at Sunday's service. It was a lovely day, and they were happy.

Suddenly, without warning, an earthquake struck. The house was shaken violently by the first tremor. Oka-san and Daishero were thrown from the open upper veranda to the garden below. Dazed and bruised, Oka-san struggled to her knees, the cries of her baby ringing in her ears. She saw that the heavy tile roof of the building had collapsed, trapping her husband in the debris. Desperately she struggled to loosen the tiles which held him, but she could not. A new tremor sent additional tiles tumbling around them, and the brave pastor urged Oka-san to leave him and save herself and the baby.

Oka-san rushed into the street, searching for someone to help her. Everywhere there was confusion, people crying out, men and women trying frantically to dig their own loved ones from the wreckage. There was no one to come to her aid.

Praying that her other children were safe and that Daishero might not be too seriously hurt, she ran back to what was left of their home and church. But her beloved husband had succumbed to his serious injuries.

Bravely, Oka-san held back her own grief and went to help the injured. News came that the school had been spared, and soon her older children—Hedeko, in her teens, Eüchi, the first-born son, and Masako, the youngest daughter—joined her. Quietly she told them of their father's death, and the little family prayed together. Then, while Hedeko cared for the baby Daishero, the others worked through the night, the children helping to clear away rubble, Oka-san tending the injured and dying.

When the disaster was over, Oka-san and her brood were homeless and without resources. For a time they managed with the help of friends, but the village had been hard hit, and there was little for anyone. Daishero, who had not seemed badly hurt, grew ill, and it was discovered that his hip had been injured. Tuberculosis set in.

Stunned by this new misfortune, Oka-san scarcely knew where to turn. Somehow she must find medical help for her baby and a way to support herself and her children. She prayed to God for help.

And help came. In Akashi, Sensei heard of the tragedy, and

her heart responded with warm generosity. That very day she traveled to the small village and brought Oka-san and the children to Sunrise Home.

"You will make your home here with us," she told Oka-san. "There is plenty for everyone, and work to do, too."

She appointed Oka-san as a matron, Hedeko as a helper. Eüchi was apprenticed to a tradesman in Akashi, and little Daishero was overwhelmed with loving care.

But it soon became apparent that Daishero was not gaining in health. He needed hospital treatment, and Sensei found a place for him in a sanitarium in Kobe. (This is where he had been for the past months.)

Now Sensei smiled gently at the children gathered around her. "There is time for each of you to pick a flower for Daishero before school," she said. Her eyes twinkled a little. *"If* your chores are all done properly!"

"They are!" the children chorused. "Oh, Sensei they are!" They assured her that the *futons* which served as bedclothing on the *tatami* mat floors had been carefully folded, that their rice bowls were washed, that the smallest children's hair had been carefully combed.

"Then each of you find one flower," Sensei smiled. "It shall be your gift."

The children spread through the garden, very much like bright flowers themselves. Each searched for the prettiest blossom she could find, and one by one they brought them to Sensei.

"Look, I have a white rose!" "See, Sensei, I have found a beautiful iris!" "I have a branch of cherry blossoms! The very last to open, so I know the Lord Jesus must have meant it for Daishero!"

Sensei gathered all the flowers together in one great bouquet.

Perhaps it was not as elegant as those achieved in the famous Japanese flower-arranging classes. Some of the smaller children's flowers had short stems, and every flower that bloomed in the garden was represented, but no bouquet ever carried more love than the one Sensei took with her when she left on the Kobe train that morning.

Little Daishero lay very still in his hospital crib. His dark eyes were shadowed with pain, and his small face pinched. Sensei's heart ached as she bent over him. He was so tiny and defenseless—and so very alone here.

She stroked his soft hair and showed him the bright flowers, talking gently about the children who loved him. "Here's a yellow one, Daishero. Eiko-san sent it. And here is a red one."

She held it out to him, and for a moment his eyes lighted up. His small hand closed around the flower, and the bright blossom nodded as he waved it back and forth. A smile touched his lips, and then suddenly he laughed, reaching out for all of the flowers. It was the first time Sensei had heard him laugh for many weeks, and tears stung her eyes. She held the flowers close, and his hands patted at them. Then, tired, he lay back, but the happiness remained in his eyes until he fell asleep.

In the conference room Sensei faced the doctor.

"Things are not going well, are they?" she asked.

He shook his head soberly.

Sensei bit her lip, looking down at her hands. Then she looked up at the doctor again, meeting his gaze squarely. "He is not going to get well, is he?" she asked.

For just a moment he hesitated, and then he said quietly: "No, Sensei. Daishero will not get well."

Sensei sat without moving. She was seeing Daishero's face

when she held the flowers toward him, seeing the hospital crib, the long ward where he lay. And she was seeing Sunrise Home with its gardens and its love, seeing Oka-san. She knew what she wanted to do.

"I want to take him home," she said. "Home to his mother. We'll care for him, doctor. "We'll give him every care."

"Sensei, I know," the doctor said, troubled. "And I wish Daishero could be with his mother, too. But you know what the disease is. You know that it's essential for the other children to be kept from contact with him."

Sensei's back straightened. "Yes, I do," she said firmly. "But I feel that Daishero is meant to be with his mother these last months. You must promise me something!"

The doctor smiled. He knew that when Sensei felt that God meant something to be, her mind would not be changed. "What do you want me to promise?" he asked.

"That if we can make the proper arrangements at Sunrise Home, you will give me permission to take him," Sensei said.

The doctor studied her. "All right," he said at last. "You have my promise. But I know Sunrise Home," he added, "And I don't see how you're going to manage."

"We'll work something out," Sensei said with conviction.

At the moment she did not know what that "something" was. All the way back on the electric train to Akashi her mind was busy with the problem. Just as they were pulling into the railroad station, a thought popped into her mind.

"The rickshaw shed!" she exclaimed out loud, and the Japanese gentleman sitting next to her turned and looked at her politely. Sensei beamed at him. "It's a splendid idea!" she announced to the bewildered passenger. "Isn't it marvelous what the Lord makes you think?"

Gathering up her purse and gloves she marched triumphantly from the train. "That poor man probably thinks I'm daft!" she chuckled to herself. But that did not bother Sensei! It was not the first time she had bewildered someone.

She could scarcely wait to reach the Home, and before she even took off her hat she was out making an inspection of the rickshaw shed. It hadn't housed a rickshaw for many years—Sensei did not approve of rickshaws. On rainy days the children used the shed for a playroom, and it was true, they would miss it. But it would do very well for Daishero and his mother. It was sturdily built and the floor was good.

She peered out the back window. "If only that mound of dirt weren't there!" she thought. "It cuts off the sunshine."

The mound was a big one—the children called it their "mountain" and romped and played on it. At the moment Sensei had no answer for the mountain. She only knew that the rickshaw shed could be made pleasant and comfortable, and that was enough for the first step.

She did not tell either Oka-san or the children immediately of her plan. The only one she confided in that afternoon was Mercy Coles, who taught Bible and piano at the Home and was Sensei's good friend.

"It's a wonderful idea!" Mercy said. "Oka-san doesn't say anything, but I know how she's been grieving. She knows, Irene. She knows Daishero is slipping away, and she longs to be with him."

Sensei's hand close over her friend's. "She will be soon!" she promised, her eyes shining.

After the evening meal, Sensei's "family" gathered about her for evening prayers, and everyone felt some new joy in Sensei's words as she spoke of the Lord. The whole room seemed to be filled with it, and the children's voices sounded particularly sweet as they sang the last hymn.

When the time of worship was over, Sensei took Oka-san aside. "I'm going to take over the duties tonight," she said. "You go to see Daishero. You can make it in plenty of time for evening visiting hours."

Oka-san's face shone. "Oh, Sensei, I should like that! He has been on my mind all this day, more than usual. *Arigato gozai-masu* . . . thank you, thank you."

"Don't thank me!" Sensei smiled. "Hurry along now. Don't miss the train."

As soon as Oka-san had gone, Sensei called the children to her. They sat in a semicircle around her, looking up expectantly into her face. Sensei leaned toward them.

"You all know that I saw Daishero today," she said, "for I told you how he smiled when he saw the flowers you sent him. I told you how he laughed, and I know that made you happy."

"Oh, yes, Sensei!" the children agreed.

Sensei looked at them seriously. "But there is more I must tell you," she said. "Little Daishero is very, very ill. I do not think he has much longer to live."

The children's eyes widened. One of the older girls made a small sound and put her hand to her lips, her eyes suddenly bright with tears. Little Fujiko, who was five, looked up at Sensei gravely.

"Is Jesus taking him home to heaven?" she asked.

Sensei nodded. "But there may be many months before Daishero goes to his heavenly home, and it is lonely for him in the big hospital so far from his mother. So I have a plan that I want to tell you."

The children looked at her eagerly. Sensei's eyes held theirs.

"I want to bring Daishero here, she said. "I want to bring him to our Home!"

Instantly the children were full of excitement. Sensei quieted them. She explained that there must be a separate place for Oka-san and Daishero.

"I thought of the rickshaw shed," she said. "But of course, that is your playhouse. Would you be willing to give it up for Daishero?"

There was a moment of surprised silence, then the children were chorusing agreement. Each one had a plan—how they would clean the floors and walls, how they would make the little shed bright and comfortable.

"If only," Sensei exclaimed, "there were some way to chop the head off your mountain and let in the sunshine!" A thought flashed through her mind. "I know what we can do!" she cried. "We can take away the mountain ourselves! Every day each one of us can take a shovelful of dirt and carry it across the road to the beach of our bathing place. We'll have it gone in no time!"

The children were entranced with the idea. Early the next morning Sensei hurried to the municipal offices in Akashi, for the mountain, as it happened, stood on property belonging to the city. A polite official gave her permission to remove it, saying that the hill was nothing but wasteland, anyway.

The work began. Sensei had Nan-san, the elderly gardener, loosen the earth at the top of the hill so that it would be easier for the children to move the dirt. Shovels were left handy. Everyone pitched in. Two of the older girls asked Nan-san to put up a wooden pole with a board nailed near the top to serve as a bulletin board. For good measure he gave the board a protective zinc roof, which made it quite grand. Every Monday morning one of the girls posted a clean sheet of paper with the names of all the children on it. When a child carried away a shovelful of dirt, it was marked down. Sensei and the other staff members carried their daily quota, too. Often the older children carried extra shovelfuls for the small ones. And Sensei knew that Oka-san who was nearly overcome with happiness, sometimes slipped out after her chores were finished and trudged back and forth with many loads of dirt.

But the "mountain" was big, and even though many shovelfuls of earth were carried away, there seemed to be little change in it. The weather grew hot and humid. The children's interest flagged no matter how Sensei tried to keep it up.

Then the third week in June—the hottest day there had been that summer—a letter from Mrs. Paget Wilkes, wife of the mission's field director, arrived. Her husband, she wrote, was suffering from high blood pressure, and the doctor had ordered him to Karuizawa, a mountain resort where the Barclay Buxtons had established a rest home for the missionaries. This would be a time, he felt, for Sensei to help him with important mission papers which his busy schedule had forced him to neglect, and he directed her to report at the resort without delay.

Sensei's heart sank. How could she leave the children in the middle of the project? Removing the mountain was even more important now than it had been at first, for the doctor had told her that he could not let Daishero leave the sanitarium unless he could have full sunshine. But Sensei knew that if Paget Wilkes thought it important for her to work on mission papers, she must go. One did not say "no" to the field director.

That evening at prayers she told the children she must leave the next day. Their faces fell. Sensei tried to encourage them. She told them she would hurry back as soon as she could, and that she knew they would do their very best with the mountain while she was gone. But the children's faces betrayed their feelings all too clearly. They were surprised and unhappy.

"Shall we pray about this?" Sensei asked.

The children nodded, and Sensei called on Eiko-san to begin. "Dear Lord," the little girl prayed. "You know all about that mountain. That mountain is slow coming down even with Sensei here. The top came off easy, but the longer we work, the harder it gets."

Reiko looked up. "I don't think that's a proper kind of prayer!" she objected.

Eiko-san looked rebellious, and Sensei hushed them. "Let us pray from our hearts," she said. "Each one as she feels."

The prayers went on. Sacheko, her small head bent over her clasped hands, prayed very earnestly. "Lord Jesus, last Sunday we heard in Sunday School that if we had faith as a grain of mustard seed, we could remove mountains. Lord, help us remove our mountain."

A little murmur ran through the group. *If they had faith. . . .*

"Dear Lord," Hanachan prayed, "You said we could move a mountain into the sea. Here the sea is just across the road. Will you please take our mountain and put it into the sea?"

Sensei felt her own faith growing stronger within her. She looked into the earnest faces of the children, and she nodded. "We will see," she said.

That night she had a special word for each child as she tucked them in. The next morning she took the early train for Karuizawa.

The mountain resort was delightful, and Sensei's quarters far more comfortable than those at Sunrise Home. Yet the very comfort and coolness was like a hair shirt to Sensei who could not keep her mind away from the mountain and the children.

She had hoped that her stay might not be longer than a week, but Paget Wilkes was not well enough to spend long hours at work, and it dragged on. A postcard came from Mercy Coles. It said little except that the children were well and everything in order.

Then, the beginning of the third week, a card came from the children themselves. "When are you coming home?" it said. "We wish you would hurry. We have a wonderful surprise for you!"

Sensei's spirits soared. She couldn't hide her excitement. Paget Wilkes looked at her quizzically. "You've been fretting ever since you came here," he said, "though goodness knows Mrs. Wilkes and I thought a stay in the mountains would be a pleasant change for you, even with work to do. Now you look as though you might soar off the mountaintop any minute. Suppose you tell me about it."

Sensei confessed the whole story. "Of course I don't *know* what the surprise is," she finished, showing him the card. "But it *might* be the mountain, now, mightn't it?"

He laughed. "I shan't speak for the Lord," he said. "But I know one thing. We must finish up these papers tonight and let you rush back to Sunrise Home. You will never rest until you find out."

The next morning Sensei was on the train heading back for Akashi. Every click of the wheels made her excitement mount. She sat bolt upright during the entire journey, her cheeks pink, her eyes behind their thick spectacles unusually bright. "You must not anticipate the Lord's will," she cautioned herself, but she could scarcely wait for the trip to be over.

She fairly flew off the train and up the little road to Sunrise

Home. She was calling to the children before she even reached the garden path, and they came tumbling from the house and yard to meet her. Oka-san ran out, her face wreathed in smiles. Miss Coles came hurrying from the back garden where she had been picking snow peas, her ancient garden hat flapping.

"Sensei! Sensei!" the children shouted. "Shut your eyes! Don't peek! Don't look until we say!"

Many little hands guided her around the house. In their eagerness, the children pushed and tugged, and Sensei nearly toppled over on the lot of them. She was out of breath and disheveled before they came to a halt.

"Now!" the children chorused, and Sensei opened her eyes. There was the rickshaw shed. There were the flower beds blooming about it. But the mountain was gone. There was not a trace of it!

Sensei laughed and cried and hugged the children who were all talking at once. "One at a time!" she cried, holding up her hands. "Tell me, how did you do it?"

"The men came!" Eiko-san cried. "Just last Friday!"

"They had lots of shovels!" Reiko shouted.

Finally Miss Coles, with plenty of help from all the children, told Sensei the story. Friday morning of the past week a truck filled with coolies and driven by a Japanese supervisor had come up the hill. They had stopped at Sunrise Home, and the men, without a word, had swarmed over the "mountain," wielding pickaxes and shovels, and loaded the dirt onto the truck. When the first load was in, they drove away, only to come back for a second and third load.

"We were dumbfounded," Mercy said. "We asked them how they had happened to come here, and where they were taking the dirt. The supervisor told us that they were filling in land where the sea had receded to make a children's playground. They needed the mountain for fill!"

"Isn't it wonderful?" Sacheko cried. "The Lord did really move the mountain!"

"And he took it to a place where other children can play now!" Eiko-san cried. "The Lord is really good, isn't He?"

Her arms stretched wide, Sensei gathered as many of the children into her arms as she could. "Very good," she said, "Oh, very, very good, my dear ones. Let us thank Him right here."

Kneeling, Sensei and the children and the staff members gave thanks to God for His loving care and for the wonderful way He had removed the mountain and carried it to the sea to bring joy to others.

Later in the week, Oka-san went to the sanitarium and brought her son home. There in the snug little house made from the rickshaw shed, she loved him and cared for him the last months of his life. Every day the children sent a handful of flowers or pictures they had drawn, and every evening they prayed for little Daishero. There was a sense of joy and reverence at Sunrise Home. Even the smallest child seemed to realize that God had heard their prayers and intervened to make Daishero's last days happy and comfortable.

For Sensei, the removal of the mountain was just one more miraculous incident in a life of prayer and faith.

2

"I Send an Angel before Thee"

"I *should* have been born in Dublin!" Irene used to say with spirit. "*Everyone* else in the family is *properly* Irish!"

Irene herself, loyal daughter of Erin though she was, and proud of her Irish ancestry, was born in the village of Connahsquay, Flintshire, Wales, on April 11, 1888. Her parents, with their four older children, had moved there the preceding year in the hope that the mild Welsh climate would benefit her father who was suffering from what doctors then called "congestion of the lungs."

Irene has only dim memories of either the picturesque village or of her father, for he died two years later, and Ellen, his widow, carrying a sixth child, returned to the home of Thomas Batt, her father. Situated at Fairview, a suburb of Dublin, the home was large and gracious, surrounded by beautiful gardens and orchards. It was a charming place for a child to grow up.

A few miles away, at Liffeyview, was her paternal grandparent's farm, and Irene and her brothers and sisters loved to visit there. Cousins and aunts and uncles always seemed to overflow the big comfortable house, and many gay times they had there together.

Some of the Webster-Smith clan were Methodists; some were Quakers, though Grandfather William attended the Anglican church. Both the Batts and the Webster-Smiths were God-fearing Protestants in a country dominated by Roman Catholics. Every Sunday the entire family attended service, whether they were at Liffeyview or Fairview, and each day there were family prayers when a portion of the Bible was read and all bowed their heads to offer thanks to God and seek His guidance for the day.

When Irene was still in grade school, her mother began to accept the attentions of a young Dublin University instructor named Paul Duffey. He was a handsome young man with dark hair and a neatly clipped mustache. He was also a Roman Catholic.

But Ellen Webster-Smith loved him, and risking stern family disapproval, she married him. Her father disinherited her and refused to see her the remaining years of his life, not even reconciling with her on his deathbed. Most of the rest of the family ostracized her.

The Duffeys moved to Cork, where Irene's stepfather had been appointed to a professorship at Queens College. They settled in a spacious home between the Anglican rectory, where the Reverend F. W. Ainley and his family lived, and the home of the Richard P. Wood family, ardent Plymouth Brethren.

"We lived between two fires," Irene recalls laughingly. "The Ainleys were devoted low church people, active in gospel work. The Woods, who had five boys, were always at me to attend *their* Sunday school. They wanted to get me converted, but I wasn't interested. I just wanted to enjoy life, and I wondered why they felt they had to take their religion so seriously!"

Irene attended the Anglican Church. Although Roman Catholic–Protestant relations were particularly tense in Cork, the Duffey home was not disrupted by religious controversy, and twelve-year-old Irene was oblivious of the strong feelings which were building up in the land.

She was a lively youngster, always full of energy, and apt to be found where there was mischief. If a prank were played at school, the headmistress was almost sure to question Irene first. If tennis balls were accidentally batted to the school gables, it was Irene who went after them. If the farmers' wives found themselves serenaded from the roof of the barn adjoining their market, Irene was usually leading the music.

One of these roof-top concerts brought her to grief, for she slipped and fell, striking an iron picket fence and injuring one of her legs severely. During her enforced period of inactivity, she used to sit propped up on pillows in the broad living room, watching people come and go in the streets.

One Sunday afternoon as she sat there, she saw the Reverend Mr. Ainley and his wife leave their home. Mrs. Ainley was pushing the pram which held her baby daughter, and the pastor was carrying a little portable organ. Irene knew they were heading for the Marina, a promenade bordering the River Lee in downtown Cork, to conduct a street meeting, and she felt a kind of contempt for them. Street preaching was foolish, she thought. All it brought was jeers and threats.

She was still sitting in her window perch an hour or so later when she saw people running from the rectory across the street to the hospital. By their faces, she knew that something was seriously wrong, and she called to her mother. Mrs. Duffey hurried next door. When she returned, she had a sad story to tell.

The Ainleys had set up their organ in the midst of strolling afternoon crowds on the Marina. It was a beautiful sunny day, with sailboats dotting the river and a soft breeze blowing. Mrs. Ainley began to play, and a crowd started to gather. A group of rowdies began to heckle the mild-mannered but spunky Anglican preacher, and when he refused to be driven away, they grew more boisterous. A stone was thrown. It struck Mrs. Ainley in the temple, felling her instantly. She was rushed to the hospital, but she died within an hour.

Irene was shocked. She felt deep sorrow for the bereft household, and there was pain in her heart over the needless killing. Yet her own concern about religion was not awakened.

It was enough, she felt, to attend church and revere God. The Ainleys' street corner meetings, like the Woods' zeal to get converts, to her seemed useless.

About a year later the Duffeys returned to Dublin, where her stepfather joined the faculty of Trinity College. The family moved into a spacious home in a good residential section, and Irene, always popular, made many new friends.

She was in her teens when she met Miss Kathleen Fry, the eldest daughter of Sir William Fry, a noted Dublin lawyer. The Frys were deeply committed Christians who attended Merrion Hall, one of the oldest of the Plymouth Brethren chapels.

Irene was never to forget her first visit to stately Wilton House, the Fry family home. It was handsomely appointed, the furnishings both rich and tasteful. Miss Fry, wearing a purple velvet afternoon frock, entered the room. Irene thought she had never seen anyone of such rank and beauty. The very room seemed to light up when she came in.

Miss Fry smiled warmly at the young visitor and asked her about school and her friends in Cork. She spoke of the Woods family, and of the Ainleys.

Then came the question that shook Irene. "Do you know the Lord Jesus Christ," Kathleen asked, "as your personal Savior and Friend?"

Irene felt her cheeks grow pink as she fumbled for an answer. If Miss Fry had asked, "Are you a Christian?" she could have answered "yes" easily, for she was sure that she loved the Lord Jesus. But this question was different. "I don't think I know Him like that," she finally blurted.

In her heart she rebelled at the question, and she wanted to get away as fast as she could. "I hope she doesn't think I'm a heathen!" she thought, squirming inwardly.

Miss Fry continued to talk to her, saying that she hoped she would get to know Irene better, and that she would like her to come to her Bible class when she returned from a trip she was making to the Continent. "You must give me your address," she said, "so that I can send you postcards."

Reluctantly, Irene gave the address, but as she hurried home she was sure that she would never attend Miss Fry's class. "I'm perfectly satisfied with being the kind of Christian I am!" she thought hotly. Still, as the days passed, she could not get Miss Fry's question out of her mind. There was something about the words "personal Savior and Friend" which held her.

In due time postcards came from Norway and Sweden, always with a brief message containing a reference to the Lord. Irene found herself thinking more and more about her new friend, and when Miss Fry returned, Irene joined her class. Often they met at Wilton House for tea, and Irene came to be convinced that everything Miss Fry embodied, a lady should be. She began to memorize verses from the Scripture and was faithful in performing assignments her teacher gave her. More and more she found herself enjoying Bible study.

Then Irene learned that her teacher had contracted tuberculosis. Everything possible was done to save her life, but her health continued to decline, and at last she died. Irene was heartbroken, and for many days as she read her little crimson leather-covered Bible and followed the *Scripture Union* reading plan, she thought of the question Kathleen had posed for her: *Do you know Him as your personal Savior and Friend?* She knew she had never faced up to the question.

One day in October, 1904, she noticed an advertisement in the *Irish Times*. It caught her attention immediately for it announced that evangelistic meetings were being conducted in the Friends' Meath Place Mission Hall in the slum area of the city.

"Fritz Wood!" she exclaimed. "Why, he lived next door to us in Cork! He can't be more than seventeen! Imagine Fritz a boy preacher!"

She had no real interest in evangelism, but she was filled with curiosity. "Let's go to hear him!" she said to her brother, Fred. Irene didn't know it, but her brother had already secretly "gone forward" a week earlier at a meeting held by another evangelist, and he needed no urging.

Fred and Irene had difficulty locating the Quaker mission,

and they arrived late. They were ushered up front, and Irene felt uncomfortably conspicuous in the plain little chapel. She was wearing a fashionable cream-colored dress under an elegant brown velvet coat, its lining trimmed with intricate blue fluting. Bangles and baubels encircled her wrists.

She soon forgot her discomfort. Fritz Wood was a fine preacher, and Irene was stirred by his sermon. When he extended a gospel invitation, asking those who wanted to know the Lord to remain, Irene asked her brother to stay.

The congregation was singing a gospel chorus, and the words seemed to be reaching out to Irene:

> "Everybody should know,
> Everybody should know,
> I have a wonderful Savior
> That everybody should know."

Irene nodded her head in time with the music and began to sing the words. The couple sitting next to her got up to leave, and before she knew it, a tall forbidding woman swooped into the pew.

"Are you saved?" she demanded bluntly. Irene drew back, and the woman gave her a disdainful look. "I can see you're not!" she said, taking in the baubels and fashionable clothes. "Not you with all your fineries and fripperies! You won't be, either!"

Anger shot through Irene, and she jumped to her feet, signaling her brother that she wanted to leave at once. At the door a gracious woman invited to her to return, and one of Fritz's brothers also spoke to her, mentioning the old days in Cork and asking her if she didn't think it was time for her to give in to the claims of Jesus Christ on her life.

She parried the question with a laugh, though inside she was seething. Then she burst out: "Oh, I'm fed up!" And with flashing eyes she described the encounter with the woman.

All the way home she fumed about "that woman," and she was still irked when she went up to her room. Her Bible was lying on the bedside table, and she picked it up and began leafing through it. A meditative mood came over her, and crossing to her desk, she took a piece of paper and wrote on it: *Savior and Friend.* For a moment she studied the phrase, then turning to her Bible, she began to look up every reference to the two words. As she checked the Scripture, the Bible started to take on new meaning, and she began to see what Kathleen Fry had meant when she spoke of "knowing" Christ. It was an intimate knowing, closer and dearer than any friendship, an inner knowing of the soul and the heart.

Irene dropped to her knees beside the bed, quietly inviting Jesus Christ to come into her heart, and a strong sense of faith surged through her whole being. That night her spiritual decision was made.

The next evening she returned to the chapel. Members were testifying, and Irene felt a deep thrill at their words. Each seemed to have a message—and each message seemed to have meaning for her. When the call came for those who had trusted the Lord Jesus Christ for salvation during the past two weeks to stand, Irene rose with the others. It was the happiest moment of her life.

Very soon after that night, Irene was engaged in Christian service every week at the Meath Place Mission Sunday School, and this was no matter of simply teaching a class! Promptly at eight o'clock on Sunday mornings, the children from the slum neighborhood arrived at the mission. The order of the day was breakfast, baths, and then Sunday school.

Helping to feed and bathe a squirming, yelling crowd of from 150 to 300 boys and girls was a new experience for Irene, to say the least! The children lined up, pushing and shoving. They came from homes where parents were still sleeping off the drunkenness of the night before, and in few of the homes was food ever left for the unkempt children. The sandwiches on the big trays—some with bread and butter, some with jam, some with a piece of ham or beef between the slices—were often the only food these children would have for the day, or longer, and it was hard for them to wait.

"Here, now!" Irene would say. "Quiet down a bit! You'll all get your fair share!"

Then, after a word of grace was spoken, the sandwiches were distributed, and the children sat at wooden tables, wolfing down every crumb and gulping the hot tea which was served with plenty of milk and sugar in it.

Then Irene and the other workers rolled up their sleeves and donned huge aprons. Group by group, the children were led, usually protesting, to rows of tubs. Plenty of soap was used. Hair was washed, and Irene and the others worked at combing the matted locks until they were free of snarls. When the children were presentable, Sunday school started, with enough husky young men on hand to keep order. Irene played the piano and taught a class of younger boys, who were more than a handful. Strenuous as the work was, she had the joy of seeing that the children with whom she worked each week were important to God—and to her.

With typical Quaker ingenuity, the directors of the Mission Hall encouraged the boys and girls to save their pennies. If a child brought a tenpence to deposit in the Sunday school bank, twopence was added by the staff to make it a shilling. When a child needed boots or new clothing, he was given an order on a Quaker store which extended a special low price.

The sad part was that often when the children bought new shoes or clothing, the parents stole them while they slept and pawned them for drink. On more than one occasion, Irene used her own pocket money to replace what they had lost.

Irene's family was not, at first, enthusiastic about her work at the mission, which they called the "Friend's Ragged School." They were afraid she would bring home dirt and disease, and probably vermin. But they were a close, loving family, and when they realized how much joy Irene found in serving, their objections ceased.

Irene found great inspiration in Quaker worship. The "advices" read each Sunday morning always impressed her, and she found herself studying the topics: "Are you careful that those in your employ have time to attend places of worship?" "Have you made out a will that will care for your family and employees?" "Is the Holy Scripture read daily in your home?"

Following the teaching of the Quakers that the sacraments of baptism and the Lord's Supper are to be observed spiritually rather than literally, Irene was never baptized. When friends sometimes asked her about this, she would say with a twinkle in her eye: "Well, you see I was baptized earlier. A sweet Irish maid we had, used to take all of us children to a Catholic Church as soon as she could sneak us out after we were born. Afterwards, she would say to Mother: 'Ma'am, I had the little one sprinkled. She's all right for eternity.' And Mother, ever-tolerant, would say: 'Well, I suppose it didn't do her any harm.' Dear Mother!"

The weeks and the months flew by. Irene, who had studied

stenography and had ambitions to be a lawyer, found employment with a noted law firm, and the work was both challenging and stimulating.

Her sisters were socially active, filling their lives with gay parties and balls. There were plenty of eligible young men courting all of the Webster-Smith girls, and Irene, with her twinkling blue eyes and chestnut colored hair, had her share of suitors. One by one the other girls married, and Irene's mother fondly predicted that Irene would soon follow in their footsteps. But Irene, engrossed in her job, her studies and her mission work, was sure that she would go on with her dream of a career as a barrister.

Ireland was torn, during these times, by the long struggle for freedom from British rule, and although Irene was not particularly interested in politics, she could not help but be somewhat involved. Her family was loyal to the Crown, and the firm where she worked was the very epitome of British overlordship. After Great Britain declared war on Germany in 1914, she was far more deeply involved. As a Quaker, she had a horror of war. Political strife and wartime restrictions drove many of Ireland's fine young men from the country. Irene's brother Will went to India. Fred, her younger brother, settled in America.

There were times during this period when Irene doubted the rightness of her wish to be a lawyer. At moments she felt that God might want her on the foreign mission field, and the pull was strong—so strong that she actually avoided going to missionary meetings or reading missionary magazines. She was afraid that she would succumb to the call.

And she had another reason for wishing to stay at home. She had fallen in love with a young man named Al Quigley, a student at Baptist Seminary in Dublin. He was a steady, good-looking boy, of excellent family, deeply devout, and very much in love with Irene. Secretly he gave her a ring—a beautiful golden one with eight little pearls and two rubies set in it—and there was a definite understanding between them. They did not make their plans public because engagements were normally two years in length, and they felt that it was not yet time to make a formal announcement.

Irene's sisters were all married now, and Irene loved to visit their homes. She daydreamed about the one she would have some day, and she and Al, walking hand in hand along shaded lanes or across the green fields, made all kinds of plans.

Irene got the feeling at this time that she was not facing up to the Lord's claims upon her life. To use a phrase she quoted from the Bible, she was "having a controversy with the Lord." Night after night she struggled with this controversy. She had told the Lord when she was converted that she must lead at least one soul to Christ each month. This she had done. But she felt guilty about avoiding missionary meetings.

"Lord," she prayed, "I *can't* go to the mission field. I'm studying law, and I'm practically engaged to Al."

The crosscurrents of her life had a devastating effect on her spiritual life. A month went by, and she did not reach a soul. A second month passed. At the testimony meetings at Meath Place, her heart felt empty. Bible study did not seem as interesting any more, and she neglected prayer. One of the elderly Quaker ladies chided her gently, but Irene could not respond. Her heart had grown cold.

She began to miss Sunday school. Almost every weekend she managed to be out of town. Finally she gave up going to the Mission Hall completely.

For six months this went on. Then on Easter Sunday in 1915,

Irene went to visit a beloved aunt and uncle at Liffeyview. She attended church that morning, and the message of the Risen Christ seemed to give her a fresh touch from the Lord. That afternoon she detached herself from the crowd of friends and relatives and went alone for a walk in the Wicklow hills. With her Bible in her hand, she began to pray, asking the Lord's forgiveness.

"Restore unto me the months the locusts and cankerworms have eaten," she prayed. "Restore unto me the joy of salvation . . . Lord, will you give me souls again?"

Alternating between reading the Scripture and praying, Irene spent the entire afternoon in the presence of the Lord.

"I will go to Timbuktu if you want me to, Lord!" she cried out in the distress of her soul. "Give me joy in Your service and use me again to win souls."

The struggle within her seemed to slip away, and a feeling of strength and calm came back to her. Weeping, she thanked God for His grace.

It was a great joy for Irene to return to her mission work and to the intimate group of friends who often met for dinner together and held prayer meetings afterwards. Following one of these meetings, the group attended a service conducted by the Japan Evangelistic Band. There were two speakers, and they spoke inspiringly of the society's work in Japan. As she left the meeting, Irene bought a copy of their magazine.

Going home on the tramcar, she found herself absorbed in an article by the Reverend Paget Wilkes, field director of JEB. It told about the work an American, Miss Christine Penrod, was doing in Tokyo for Japanese prostitutes. Japan's brothels were government licensed and exceedingly profitable. Thousands of young women were trapped in the vicious system, and Miss

Penrod was working desperately to rescue young country girls from the vice network. The last sentence in the article read: "Is there not someone in England who would go out and do secretarial work to help this lady for two years?"

Irene felt as though the message was directed straight at her. She caught her breath and her hands closed on the magazine. The realities of the tramcar slid away, and she saw herself working in the Rescue Home. She was sure she had received her call from God.

When she got home, she went straight to her mother's room. Mrs. Duffey had already retired, and Irene sat down on the edge of her bed. She held the magazine in her hands.

"I've been reading an article in this magazine, Mother," she said. "I believe it has shown me the call of God."

Her mother smiled fondly at her daughter. "Has it, dear? I'm sure that's very nice."

Irene drew in a quick breath. "Mother, I believe that God wants me to go to Japan and serve there."

Mrs. Duffey sat up abruptly. "Nonsense, child!" she said. "You can't go to Japan!"

"Mother, I don't want to go against your wishes," Irene said earnestly, "but I feel I must be obedient to whatever He shows me. Please, Mother, read the article."

Her mother took the magazine and put it aside without glancing at it. "You can't go to Japan, Irene," she said firmly. "You're needed here, and that's the end of that."

"But Mother," Irene persisted. "My sisters have left home. They've married. . . ."

"And I won't object to your leaving when you marry," her mother said. She smiled brightly at Irene. "I won't say no to

Al when he asks you. Now run along to bed, and let's hear no more about this."

Silently Irene left the room. In her own room, she opened *Daily Light* and read the portion for the day: "Behold I send an angel before thee to prepare the place and to bring thee into the place which I have prepared for thee."

Thoughtfully, Irene read the verse again, and then after her prayers, she slipped into bed. The word "Japan" seemed to be written on her heart.

The next morning her mother called her to her room before breakfast. Her face looked thin, Irene thought, and there was something in her eyes Irene could not read. She put out her hand to her daughter and drew her close.

"I'm sorry about last night, child," she said. For a moment she was silent, her hand quiet on Irene's. Then she spoke again. "I was taken up with my own concerns last night, Irene. I didn't listen to yours."

"I understand, Mother," Irene said.

Her mother looked at her, studying her face, seeing the earnestness and the hope there, and something deeper than that.

"I read the article last night after you had left me," she said slowly. "And if this call is to you, then I know you must answer it."

Irene's heart beat fast. "I know that it is, Mother! I'm sure."

Her mother nodded. "You will go to Japan," she said quietly. And then she added: "But not until after I have gone Home."

The color drained from Irene's face. "Mother, what do you mean?" she gasped. "You're a young woman! You're only in your fifties!" Alarm tightened her voice. "Mother, is there something . . . ?"

Her mother shook her head, silencing her. "I don't know, Irene. But I feel that's what God showed me last night after you had left me. You will go to Japan after I have gone Home."

Something in her mother's voice, something in her face, stopped Irene from any questions or arguments. Words she might have said were stilled at her lips. Her hand tightened suddenly on her mother's, and they sat together for a long moment.

That was on November 12, 1915. In the months that followed Irene continued her work at Meath Place. She found joy in the work, and fulfillment, but the thought of Japan was never out of her mind. She did not speak of it, even to Al. But when he suggested that they announce their engagement, she put him off gently.

"Wait a little, Al," she asked him. "Wait a little more."

She and her mother were strangely close during those months. They did not speak of what had been said that night, but there was a bond between them which had not been there before. Irene saw her mother grow thinner. Sometimes she now saw pain shadowing her face, yet in her eyes there was a new serenity.

By midsummer Mrs. Duffey was no longer able to leave her bed, for the cancer which none of the family had known about for so long, had made great inroads. On August 15 she slipped quietly away. Irene felt the sorrow in her heart, but some of the pain of parting had been removed on that day months before, and she felt that the Lord was moving in her life in strange and mysterious ways.

"He said He would send an Angel before me," she whispered.

"I didn't know it would be the Angel of Death."

As soon as possible, she wrote to the Japan Evangelistic Band, and a reply came by return mail. The opening in Tokyo was still waiting. She was the only one who had applied.

The mission officials suggested that she take some work at the Faith Mission Bible College in Edinburgh. She enrolled in January, 1916, and remained until the following June. While at the school she also worked with underprivileged children. It was like carrying on at Meath Place.

"They come to us in rags and barefooted, even in the dead of winter," she wrote to Al. "We bathe them and give them clothing and shoes. Sometimes we are called upon to settle domestic problems in their homes, and we spend many hours calling on the sick and lonely people. Part of the time I help out in a Sunday school for girls who sell fruit and vegetables."

In June the annual Japan Evangelistic Band conference was held at Swanwick, England. Irene was invited to appear before the mission council. A group of her cronies went with her, and they sat on the stairs of the building as Irene went up for her examination.

"I never saw such a council meeting in my life!" Paget Wilkes, who was chairing the meeting, said later. "There were several ladies there—including my wife—and all of them were close friends of Irene's. Instead of questioning the candidate, they began to embrace Irene and tell her how glad they were she was joining the Band!"

The appointment to serve with Miss Penrod was for two years. In her heart, Irene thought that at the end of that time she would return and marry Al, but she felt it unfair to hold him to their understanding.

"I want you to take back your ring," she told him.

Al protested vigorously. He was still a seminary student, and he knew it was inadvisable for him to marry until he had completed his course and been called to a church, and he was not against Irene's going to Japan, but he cherished the thought that when she returned in two years they would be married.

"I don't think it's fair to tie you up," Irene said.

"I'll tie myself up!" Al told her, insisting that she keep the ring.

Reluctantly, Irene agreed. But in her heart she had many misgivings. She did not know what the future would bring.

3

Ordeal at Jiaikwan

The year 1916 was a violent one. The simmering movement for Irish freedom boiled over in the Easter Rising, which spelled the end of British authority and the founding of the Irish Republic.

Britain was locked in a life and death struggle with Germany. On May 31 the Battle of Jutland, the greatest sea battle the world had ever known, marked the beginning of Germany's devastating submarine warfare.

Irene found it extremely difficult to obtain passage to Japan. For weeks she went to shipping offices, only to be turned down again and again. Finally she managed to book passage on the *Suwa Maru*, a Japanese freighter.

She boarded the vessel October 9 at Tilbury, just east of London. The ship stole quietly out of the Thames and picked its way cautiously through the English Channel which was teeming with submarines.

The passengers, largely missionaries and their families bound for African and Far Eastern ports, were not allowed on deck. They exercised by walking up and down the darkened passages of the *Suwa Maru*, and ebullient Irene Webster-Smith, who had a talent for meeting new people and new situations, started shipboard games and was generally in the center of any fun that went on. Some of the older missionaries tightened their lips in disapproval, but the fledgling missionary did not believe that one had to be dour to be sincerely dedicated to God's work.

The ship docked at Capetown in three weeks, and Irene spent several days with missionaries of the Africa Evangelistic Band, stationed at Claremont. Then the long journey was resumed. Passengers were allowed more freedom now, and Irene conducted Sunday school classes for the children, two of whom confessed their faith in Christ. At other times she talked to the Japanese sailors, trying to learn something about their difficult language. She managed to memorize five thousand words during the three months' voyage.

On the morning of December 2, 1916, the *Suwa Maru* docked at Kobe. Irene had finally reached Japan!

A first-term missionary, named Godfrey Foster, met her and helped her through customs and escorted her to the Band's headquarters. Irene was excited, trying to absorb everything at once. It was all so different from London and Dublin. The noisy crowds of men, women and children in brightly colored kimonos, the cries of the street hawkers, the open stalls, and strange smells—all were intriguing.

"Why are the streets decorated?" Irene asked.

"They knew you were coming," Foster grinned. Then he explained that the Japanese, who regard Christmas as a commercial celebration, always decorate their streets for the holiday.

At the headquarters, Irene was warmly greeted. A letter from Barclay Buxton, the Band's founder, was waiting to welcome her, and Irene felt that at last she was truly a member of the JEB.

On Sunday she went with the others to the huge Mission Hall in downtown Kobe, where she listened to a three-hour sermon in Japanese. The five thousand words she had learned from the sailors did not help her understand it, and she found later that a good many of those words would not be used in church or anywhere else! That evening she squatted on the Mission Hall floor, sitting on her feet Japanese style, for a three-hour Christmas program. She had really been initiated!

After Christmas, she traveled to Tokyo, where she had been assigned to stay with the Reverend and Mrs. George Braithwaite while studying the language. The day-long journey was a delight. It seemed to Irene that for hours the train circled around peerless, snow-capped Mount Fuji which rose majestically against a beautiful blue sky. From time to time she had glimpses of the Pacific Ocean and the beautiful coastline, and she felt that Japan was, indeed, a land of enchantment.

She was greeted at the Tokyo station by two new missionaries who had been in the field only a few months. One was Miss Grace Mosley, the other, Adelaide Soal, a young woman in her late twenties, slender, dark-haired and wearing glasses perched on her aquiline nose. She had left her post as a high school teacher in Carlisle, England, to serve the Lord in Japan. She and Irene were soon to become boon companions and co-workers.

In the overwhelming confusion of the great Oriental city,

Irene was glad to have the companionship of her two colleagues. They were drawn through the crowded streets in rickshaws to the modest Braithwaite home. Mr. Braithwaite, a burly Englishman with an austere mien and a warm heart, was secretary of the Japan Book and Tract Society for which he was then engaged in extensive translation work. His wife, a reserved Scottish woman, was a member of the JEB council, and taught a Bible class at Miss Penrod's Rescue Home, where Irene was to work.

But before that work started, Irene was taken by Mrs. Braithwaite to spend the rest of the holiday season at the seaside town of Hayama, a beautiful resort where the Imperial Family had its winter palace. The Braithwaites had a small house there, almost adjoining the palace grounds. From the window there was a magnificent view of the ocean and shoreline with Mount Fuji silhouetted against the sky. It was a lovely setting for Irene's real introduction to the Land of the Rising Sun, and she and Mrs. Braithwaite took long walks into the hills, tramping through country villages and discovering lookouts that disclosed new vistas of the picture-book landscape.

After the lovely days at Hayama, Irene returned to Tokyo with Mrs. Braithwaite. To her deep disappointment, she learned that she could not enroll in the language school in the middle of the year. It was frsustrating to realize that she could not join her new friends. Instead she had to engage a tutor who came an hour a day four days a week—quite a contrast to the five hours daily her fellow missionaries were receiving!

Early in January, Irene made her first trip to Miss Penrod's Rescue Home for prostitutes. Situated in Okubo in the outskirts of Tokyo, the Home was named "Jiaikwan." In Japanese, *Ji* means mercy; *ai,* love; and *kwan,* a large house. Thus it was the Home of Mercy and Love.

Miss Penrod, about whom Irene had read so long ago, was a huge amazon of a woman with wavy white hair and a great capacity for work. She had come to Japan from Nebraska, with a do-gooder's idea of a missionary's endeavor. Some time after she had reached Japan, she heard Paget Wilkes preach on the prodigal son and later on the woman of Samaria, and for the first time she learned what it meant really to trust in Christ. She resigned from the society which had sent her overseas and continued to work under the aegis of the JEB.

Irene could not begin full-time work at Jiaikwan until she had a better grasp of the Japanese language, but she devoted an afternoon a week to helping Miss Penrod with secretarial work, and even this small contact with the Rescue Home made her appreciate the desperate importance of the work. She felt more than ever that she had surely been called to this service, and she was convinced in her heart that the understanding she and Al had must be broken. She wrote him, telling him of her very strong feelings, and she returned his ring to him.

Irene studied diligently during the weeks that followed. She kept her nose buried in a pocket Japanese-English dictionary. She memorized Scripture verses in Japanese. At church gatherings, at services in Akasaka Hospital where she played the organ, at prayer meetings, she kept her ears tuned to the peculiar idioms of the difficult Japanese language. She started trying to translate "Helps to Holiness," a book by Commissioner Brengle of the Salvation Army, but this proved very difficult.

"I think I'll call it 'Hindrances to Holiness,' " she joked, making a face.

In the spring, Mrs. Braithwaite took ill and had to be hospitalized. Irene was left in full charge of the household, and this very circumstance forced her to speak Japanese constantly.

When she went to the meat market, if she didn't know the names of the meats hanging in the open shop, she would ask the butcher, "What's that?" He would answer in Japanese, and she would try to memorize the name.

She followed the same formula when she visited the vegetable and fruit stalls, bought stamps at the Post Office, visited the apothecary shop, or shopped for household items. Soon most of the shopkeepers of the Akasaka district knew the friendly missionary who was learning to speak Japanese with an Irish accent!

Being in charge of the Braithwaite home was helping Irene learn more than the language. Back in Dublin, her mother and sisters had done all the housework, and Irene knew nothing about supervising a kitchen or managing a household. She soon found that making a home run smoothly took skill and time. Some of the Japanese customs did not make her learning easier. She found, for instance, that when a servant or tradesman turned his palms out and seemed to be waving her away, he was actually beckoning for her to come towards them. When she noticed a maid sweeping the stairs from the bottom step upward, and asked her why, the woman answered in surprise: "There is always more dirt on the bottom step!"

"It's a topsy-turvy land!" Irene said to Adelaide. "Just yesterday in the rain I noticed two ladies greeting one another. They put down their umbrellas and removed their scarves before bowing to each other! I don't think I'll ever learn all there is to know!"

Adelaide laughed. "Well, one thing is sure," she said,

"You're more fluent in Japanese than those of us who've been studying at school. I wish I could manage as well as you do."

During her weeks of running the household and preparing herself for work at the Rescue Home, Irene discovered several books which were of great inspiration to her. One was by Amy Carmichael, a famous missionary to India, who had originally come to Japan with Barclay Buxton and his Band, and who had worked in the country over a year. The little book, called "Sunrise Land," told of the trials and victories of missionary work in the Land of the Rising Sun, and Irene was more than delighted to discover it. In a way it was like meeting an old friend, for as a child she had read another book by Miss Carmichael, *Lotus Buds*, and had been so impressed by it that she had regularly sent gifts from her allowance to Donahvur in South India where the author-missionary had established a home for little girls rescued from lives of vice. Miss Carmichael had sent her a number of letters, and Irene had always treasured them.

Now she read *Sunrise Land* with increased interest and found that it had deep meaning for her, as did the biography of George Muller, who ran an orphanage in Bristol, England. Muller vowed that he would never express his needs to anyone but God, and Irene found herself thinking often of this vow.

She read, too, at this time, three big volumes by Paget Wilkes, the JEB field director. One was *The Dynamics of Faith*, one *The Dynamics of Redemption*, and the third *The Dynamics of Service*. The last Irene felt to be of unusual value, and she and Adelaide Soal spent many hours discussing it.

By the end of the summer of 1917, Irene was ready to begin full-time work at the Rescue Home. But before that work began, she and a group of other missionaries were sent for a rest to the lovely mountain resort of Karuizawa. Barclay Buxton had been very wise in establishing this home, for he knew how hard the missionaries labored and how exhausting their work could be. The mountain air at Karuizawa was fresh and clear and provided a respite from the soggy heat of Tokyo and other lower-lying regions. A week or two in the rest home's invigorating atmosphere enabled the JEB workers to return to service refreshed and renewed.

Anxious as she was to be at work, Irene welcomed the holiday. There were many happy excursions into the surrounding hills, many pleasant outings and picnics. And there were many opportunities for both group worship and private meditation.

Towering over Karuizawa loomed the peak of Mount Asama, an active volcano. The smoke rising from its cone could be seen by day, and at night its fires lighted the skies. Irene, always adventurous, was eager to climb the volcano, and her enthusiasm was catching.

A climbing party, led by two missionaries who had climbed the mountain many times, were to leave on a beautiful August day, so Irene and Adelaide joined that party. They tramped until nightfall when they reached the rim of the volcano. Cautiously they peered into the roaring cauldron. Fumes drove them back, gasping and coughing. The whole scene was eerie.

Only a few of the climbers reached the summit. All but seven went back by the path they had come. Irene and Adelaide followed the expedition's leader to get another view of the cauldron. Accompanied by Jim Cuthbertson, the two women missionaries looked in vain for another path down, but they found they were lost.

The strange volcanic region seemed to have no landmarks. Shouts to the others brought no response. In vain they searched for the path to Karuizawa. Apprehension gave way to near panic, and they knew how worried Jim's wife, Clara, and the others must be. In desperation they continued to walk, not knowing that in the darkness they were moving in circles. The black lava of the mountain was sharp and treacherous. They ached with fatigue, and then when it seemed to Irene and Adelaide that they could not possibly walk another foot, they stumbled onto the path. Overwhelming relief washed over them, and in breaking dawn they plunged down the path, slipping and sliding, sometimes falling, but carried forward by the realization that they would soon be back with the others. Just as they approached the resort, they saw coming towards them a band of rescuers, pulling carts with shafts at either end. The two exhausted missionaries were quickly helped into the carts and taken back to the rest home where the others, who had spent the night in fearful waiting, rejoiced to see them.

At the end of the week, Irene and the others headed back to their posts. At the Braithwaite home, two things waited for her. One was an invitation to the annual Imperial Garden Party at Akasha Palace. The other a packet and letter from Dublin.

Irene read Al's letter first. He refused to take back the ring, he said. He still felt that there was an understanding between them, and that when Irene's two years of service and his studies were completed, they would be married.

She felt a great warmth for Al sweep over her. If she were to marry, she knew that she could have no better husband than he would be, nor one she would cherish more. She did not really plan to stay beyond three years in Japan, yet she could not countenance an official engagement. She took writing paper from her desk and penned a short note to Al, telling him again that she could not wear his ring. Then, without opening the packet, she rewrapped it and mailed it back to him, thinking that the little circlet of gold and pearls and rubies had spent most of the past eight months traveling back and forth across the seas.

The Garden Party invitation she accepted. The Buxtons, with their strong vision of reaching Japanese leadership for Christ, encouraged their missionaries to attend functions of this kind because it brought them into contact with influential Japanese people.

Adelaide had an invitation to the party, too, and the girls talked eagerly of the coming event. There was a nip in the air the day of the party. Irene wore a gray whipcord suit and a large picture hat which was very becoming to her. Adelaide was dressed in a pale blue suit, and brown silk gloves with matching hat. They felt very elegant when they set off. It never occurred to them to hire a carriage. "We always traveled on shanks' mare," Irene recalls.

They were received at the inner gates of the Palace by the chamberlains and their wives and escorted through the beautifully undulating grounds of the chrysanthemum show. A feast of color met their eyes: blooms of palest yellow, gold, crimson, and darkest red; others from pale mauve to deep purple. There were flowers so huge that they were supported on thick white paper circles. Some plants were on wire frames and had perhaps a hundred blossoms on a single stem. There were cascades of tiny button-sized blooms in every shade and color.

Before the girls had seen half enough, the guests were formed into two lines, six feet apart. Many of the Japanese guests were arrayed in formal kimonos which rivaled the flowers. The ladies had high coiffures, formally arranged and lacquered.

A herald of the court marched through the aisle between the two lines. He was followed immediately by the Emperor in full regimentals. Next, at a little distance, came his Empress, wearing a long western style dress of *eau de nile* ninon and a Queen Mary style hat with ostrich feathers. The Empress was bowing to the guests on either side.

The Imperial couple was followed by the court lords and ladies clad in thick silk-padded kimonos which came right down to the ground. The ladies' long straight black hair hung almost to their kimono hems and was tied with knots of white paper. Following them came gentlemen in frock coats and tall silk hats and ladies wearing black kimonos embroidered or hand-painted from waist down.

The royal couple was escorted to a raised dais. Irene and Adelaide were invited to share a table with a court lady and her husband, who engaged them in gracious conversation. They were served a repast of turkey, ham, and cold meats. For dessert there was ice cream and coffee. Irene could not help but feel surprised.

"I thought we'd have lotus blossoms or roast peacock or something!" she whispered to Adelaide.

But the affair was delightful, and the girls chattered about it all the way home. They were somewhat disconcerted the next day to read in one of the English-language newspapers that "the two foreigners had been dressed a little plain for a Royal Garden Party!"

The Garden Party, if not forgotten, was tucked away among other memories, for both Irene and Adelaide were now assigned full time to the Rescue Home.

Jiaikwan consisted of a walled compound in which there were four main buildings—a maternity building, a clinic where diseased women received medical treatment, the staff dormitory, and a bakery. In addition there were gardens and chicken houses, and homes for the inmates. Usually there were from sixty to eighty women living within the compound.

The work was hard and the hours long. Miss Penrod proved to be something of a chore master, though she herself worked harder than anyone. There were menial tasks to do, the endless details of running the clinic and maternity wards, classes to teach, and rehabilitation work to carry out. The inmates were taught to make bread and to care for the chickens. Eggs and bread were sold from house to house to help maintain the Home.

Irene and Adelaide pitched in with a will. Weeks flew past, and it seemed that they lost all track of time. Sometimes the days seemed to run together so that a whole week had passed before the young missionaries realized it.

Every effort was made not only to teach the women useful work so they could support themselves when they left the Home, but to lead them to a knowledge of Christ. Irene and the others conducted daily Bible classes and taught the girls Christian hymns and gospel songs. They held frequent prayer meetings and every Sunday took all of the inmates to a near-by church service.

As time passed, Irene learned how discouraging the work could be. So many of the girls seemed untouched by the missionary's efforts. They came to the compound when they found they were pregnant, for they knew the maternity ward was clean, that they would get food and care. They came for medical treatment when they found they were diseased. But all too often after the unwanted baby had been born and placed in an orphanage by the missionaries, or when the disease had been cured, they slipped away.

"I can always tell when one of them is planning to run off," Irene said wearily to Adelaide one afternoon when they stopped work long enough to have a cup of tea. "She always sings the hymns the most lustily or tries to convince us of her piety. She'll be the one who is planning to escape and go back to her old habits."

Nearly every morning at breakfast some face would be missing. In spite of the compound walls and the watchful staff members, the girls found ways to get out. Sometimes they would tie their long sashes to the veranda and slip down to the ground. Then they would climb over the wall and be gone.

"They tell us that they're tired of their lives of vice," Adelaide said, shaking her head. "but the patterns they have learned seem to hold them in an iron grasp. It seems impossible for them to return to a normal life."

"If only we could reach them before they start their lives in the brothels," Irene mused. But she did not pursue the thought then. The immediate work was much too pressing.

Miss Penrod and another of the older missionaries took Irene and Adelaide on a tour of the Yoshewara vice district of Tokyo, and it was an experience neither one of them would ever forget. The brothels which lined the streets had deep verandas from which a man could look through slatted walls to pick the girl of his choice. Those which did not have such slatted walls posted large pictures of the girls outside.

At one brothel which they passed, a young British sailor was just getting out of a rickshaw. He was a fine looking man, attractive in his uniform. As he approached the house, a row of girls richly dressed in beautiful kimonos, their faces heavily made up, their perfume delicate, sat on their heels bowing low. "Welcome back," they said. It was all too evident that the young man had been there before, and Irene could not help but think how the boy's mother would feel if she knew what was going on. It sickened her.

The whole district depressed her. She could not forget the ugliness and the depravity, the rampant, licensed and police-protected vice, and she redoubled her efforts to bring the unfortunate women who were victims of the system to Christ.

Whenever anyone expressed to Irene the commonly held idea that geisha girls are not involved in vice, she contradicted them firmly.

"The rule of a geisha's life," she said, "is that they must not refuse a man anything. The geishas are trained from childhood to play the *samisen* or some other musical instrument. They learn dancing and singing, and the art of conversing with male partners. But the ultimate end of a geisha's life is immorality of some kind.

"No man ever takes his wife to a party where geishas entertain. He wants his wife to be retiring, to live in the background, to look after him and his children. To be a housekeeper. In a geisha girl, he wants everything that he does not expect in his wife.

"A girl may start out as a well-trained geisha, full of charm and beauty, but the inevitable end of such a life is to become a wealthy man's mistress, or a common prostitute."

There were geisha girls in the Tokyo Rescue Home, but the greater percentage of the inmates were young girls, brought to the city with promises of beautiful clothes and an easy life. Trapped by their desire for lovely gowns and jewelry, they soon found themselves in debt to their owners, and working for brothel keepers who had no intention of letting them go so long as they were young and pretty.

Irene had a very good example of the lengths to which a brothel keeper would go to keep an attractive girl in the vice net. Not long after she had made the tour of the vice district, a beautiful young girl came to the Rescue Home, begging the missionaries to help her escape from the life she had been trapped into. They took her in and let her stay at the staff house—she was terrified for fear she would be seized and dragged back to the brothel.

The next day when Irene came home from a shopping trip for Miss Penrod, she found a lot of rough-looking men and police in front of the Home. They were looking for the girl, and they demanded her return.

Irene pretended not to understand them. She went along the path to the house, stopping to talk to the cook's twin boys who were playing with her parasol. One of the policemen strode up and grabbed her by the shoulder, turning her roughly to him.

"Do you think we have nothing to do but wait while you play with children?" he demanded furiously. "We are going to search the house!"

Irene said nothing. She only hoped that the staff had somehow managed to conceal the girl. Her lips set in a straight line, she went on to the house, stopping in the entrance to remove her shoes. The policeman forged past her up the stairs, slid open the doors, and found the room empty.

Irene, her heart fluttering, went into the house. The policeman marched across the sitting room, looking sharply at a cluster of girls there, and continued on through the house, slamming doors and shouting questions which no one answered. He stomped back to Irene, his face more enraged than ever. "Where is she?" he demanded, shaking her roughly.

Irene pointed to a room, and he pulled the door open and looked in. The room was empty and the window open.

"She has escaped!" Irene said on the spur of the moment, though she had no real idea where the girl was.

The policeman was beside himself, so furious that as he rushed from the house he gave Irene a shove which made her fall. She was only shaken up, and as she got to her feet she could hear the shouts from outside as the police and the other men rushed off in search of their lost prize. Irene hurried to the back rooms, anxious to know what had happened.

The policeman ran down the garden path and passed an old woman jogging a baby on her back. It took Irene a long moment to realize that the "old woman" was actually the young girl whom her friends had quickly disguised. The angry policeman had gone past her without even a look.

There were other times that the police and the brothel keepers came to reclaim girls when even Miss Penrod could not hide them, and Irene grieved for each lost girl, just as she did for those who slipped over the wall at night to return to their old ways. But there were joyous times, too—times when a girl took Christ into her life and accepted Him as her Savior and Friend, and these times were deeply moving and rewarding.

So engrossed was Irene in her work, so full her days, that she was startled at the approach of her second Christmas at Jiaikwan. It did not seem possible that so many months could have passed. She realized almost blankly that the war in Europe had ended and the Armistice been signed. Somehow it seemed remote and unreal. She realized, too, that she could return home now. The two years she had promised to give were up, but she knew that she did not want to leave. The work was far too important, her dedication to it far too deep.

She wrote to Al telling him that she must stay on, and in due course she received a letter from him saying that he understood and would not press her to return before she felt the time was right. The same mail brought a small package from him, larger than the familiar ring box, and Irene opened it, wondering what it could be. She found two small boxes within the package, and when she opened them, she saw her ring in one, and in the other an identical ring in a man's size. There was a note, too, saying that he had sent both rings because he wanted her to see them and the message which he had had engraved within each. He asked her to wear one ring and to return the other so that he could wear it. Irene took the rings and looked at the engraving. It was the Mizpah blessing: "The Lord watch between me and thee while we are absent one from another."

Silently Irene put the rings back in their boxes. She picked up the paper, meaning to turn it fresh-side-out and return the rings. But then she paused. If she sent the rings back, would not Al, faithful and loving as he was, wear the ring he had had made for himself and return the other to her again? She was sure this is what he would do, no matter what she wrote to him. Better for her to keep both rings. Perhaps then he would accept the fact that there could not, at this time, be even an informal understanding between them. With a small sigh, Irene wrapped the two white boxes in the paper they had come in and unlocking her trunk put them inside it. Then she locked the trunk again and went downstairs to prayer meeting.

In the third year of her work at the Rescue Home, Irene spent an increasing amount of time with the youngsters who lived in the compound, though this did not meet with Miss Penrod's fullest approval. Unconsciously, Irene was preparing for her future ministry with children. The little folk at Jiaikwan loved her, and she never was too busy to give them attention. She knew their little ways and how to deal with them.

On many occasions she was in charge of the cook's twin baby sons while their mother was busy in the kitchen, and sometimes to keep them quiet she gave them crusts of bread.

One day she cut the crusts of bread and left them on the breadboard while she went into another room to confer with Miss Penrod. When she returned, the twin boys came running with half-eaten crusts. Irene slapped their hands gently and explained that they should not take the bread until it was given to them.

The next morning, she again left the crusts on the board. When she returned to the room, the twins were just taking the crusts from the table. When they saw her, they bobbed their heads to the floor to say they were sorry.

But she caught them taking bread a third time, and this time they dropped the crusts on the floor, toddling quickly and guiltily from the room.

"I knew then they understood what sin was," she said in recounting the story to Adelaide. "I brought them back to the dining room, and although it nearly made me cry to do it, I whacked their little hands and made them each stand in a corner. They howled for a while, and then they came to me and bobbed their heads to the floor and said they were sorry. This time I knew they really meant it. I prayed with them, asking Jesus to forgive them, and they said 'Amen' at the end of the prayer. I never knew them to steal after that."

Not all of the youngsters in the compound were the children of staff members. Some belonged to mothers saved from the brothels. And some came to them in other ways.

One of these was a little twelve-year-old orphan girl, Shige San, whose name ironically means "Prosperity." The little waif had been turned out of the home of relatives, and she had made her own wretched way, sleeping under verandas and beneath the straw charcoal bags in outhouses. She stole food when she could and other times rummaged in garbage cans for meals. Finally a Japanese evangelist found her and brought her to the Rescue Home.

Miss Penrod threw up her hands. "We don't have room!" she said. "This is not a children's mission!"

But Irene, who already had her heart set on keeping the child, used her Irish charm and finally wheedled Miss Penrod into letting Shige San stay.

Shige San acted like a hunted animal. She would not speak, refused to answer questions, and made faces which seemed to say: "I don't believe you!" She grabbed the food Irene offered her and wolfed it down as fast as she could, as if she feared Irene might take it away from her. At night when the others were in bed, she would steal down to the kitchen and grab handfuls of cooked rice or whatever she could find. She could not believe that there would be food for her the next day. She had spent too many days going hungry.

Irene worked slowly and patiently with the child, gaining her trust little by little, giving her care and love and attention. Gradually the child began to respond to this love as a flower opens to the sunshine. She became Irene's little shadow, and she would sit for hours watching Irene at her chores, or listening to stories she told her of the love of Jesus.

In spite of the care given to her, the child's health, undermined by her former existence, did not improve, and finally the doctor told Irene that Shige San must be isolated from the others to protect them.

Irene did not know how she would manage, but she asked Miss Penrod for a room in the upstairs section of the clinic.

"You'll be wanting a whole house for your waifs next!" Miss Penrod said tartly. But her gruffness was only skin deep, and she gave Irene permission to use the room she wanted.

Irene spent as much time with little Shige San as she could, and the whole staff lavished care on her. But there was no hope for recovery.

One day near the end of her life she told Irene that she wanted Jesus as her Savior, and Irene rejoiced with her. In the days that followed she grew weaker and weaker, but her thin little face was always wreathed in a smile.

"I am waiting to go to Jesus," she told Irene. "When I do go, please sing 'Enter in at the Narrow Gate.' "

Irene promised, and the night little Shige San died, the staff, Miss Penrod included, gathered at her bedside and softly sang the hymn she had requested. There were tears in many eyes that night.

The child's death had a profound effect on Irene, and she wrote to her young friends back in Ireland: "Little Shige San was only one of the many hundreds of lambs in Japan whom the Good Shepherd is longing to save and bless. Won't you boys and girls who have known about the loving Savior ever since you were babies help by your prayers to bring the good news to every little child in the Land of the Rising Sun?"

As her third year of service stretched into the fourth, Irene thought more and more about the plight of the children—unwanted waifs like Shige San, fatherless babies born to the prostitutes, children given in their early years to brothel keepers, for these unprincipled men often went to poor farmers who had too many mouths to feed and in oily tones promised to educate their daughters, give them good homes, and find them good husbands. All too often the farmers believed them, and it seemed almost incredible to the ignorant peasants that such good fortune could have come to their daughters! Willingly, they turned the little girls over to the gross vice lords, thanking them profusely and bowing low to their "benefactors." The "good homes" turned out to be training grounds for the brothels, and the "husbands," the men who patronized them.

"Oh, if I could only snatch every child away from those lying villains!" Irene burst out to Adelaide. "How I'd rejoice then!"

But at Jiaikwan there was only room for a limited number of children, and the press of work among the prostitutes left only a certain number of hours to give to them. Even Irene, indefatigable as she was, could not stretch those hours further, and the plight of the children remained unsolved.

In the spring of 1920, a noted evangelist, Dr. Reuben A. Torrey, came to the Rescue Home to hold a series of meetings for the women. His visit caused a stir of excitement among the girls, not entirely for evangelistic reasons, Irene thought wryly. The meetings were a change from routine, and the girls flocked to the meetings, singing with zeal, responding with enthusiasm.

Duties kept Irene from attending the last meeting, but the next morning at breakfast, Dr. Torrey exclaimed: "Oh, you should have seen them last night! It was really the Holy Spirit at work! Many tears were shed! Those girls really came through to victory last night!"

"Isn't that grand!" Irene exclaimed, her eyes shining. "If *only* we would have a good earthquake or something to rattle them into the Kingdom while they're well saved, that would do it!"

Dr. Torrey was shocked. Miss Penrod's back stiffened. But Adelaide couldn't help but smile. She knew the girls all too well and knew what Irene had meant, too. She tried to sooth Dr. Torrey by explaining how quickly and easily the girls could backslide once the emotion of the moment had passed.

"Well," he said, somewhat weakly, "we must trust in the Lord, mustn't we?"

Shortly after this, almost like a grim fulfillment of Irene's impulsive exclamation, an epidemic of Spanish influenza swept the Rescue Home. It was part of the world-wide epidemic which was fatal to a million Japanese alone.

The terrible disease struck down the inmates of the Rescue Home one after another. Irene and the others worked day and night, tending the sick. The hospital was jammed. Cots lined the corridors. Nothing, it seemed, would halt the devastating progress of the pestilence.

For weeks the missionaries worked, Miss Penrod at the helm. Often they served round the clock, doing all they could to help the stricken women physically, talking to them of Christ's proferred healing for their souls. Many of the dying confessed Him as Savior.

In spite of every effort to keep the dormitory clean, there was simply not time. The police took to bringing sick prostitutes found in the streets to Jiaikwan, and they were often infested with vermin. Body lice threatened to take over the place. As soon as a woman died, the lice would leave the corpse and move to the nearest living woman. The missionaries fought off the lice, using kerosene in their battle. Their bodies stung from it, but as Adelaide said, that was better than the itching caused by lice. One day Irene, who had just doused herself again, looked up wearily at Adelaide.

"Do you know," she said blankly, "we've been going for

ten days without changing our clothes. No wonder we're lousy!"

But there was no time to bathe and change clothes. The missionaries snatched moments of rest when they could, falling across their beds for a half hour of sleep, then going back to their labors.

Tokyo was paralyzed by the epidemic. There were not enough doctors and nurses to go around. The undertakers ran out of coffins. The missionaries could not get corpses to the crematories and officials had to take bodies to hastily dug pits and cover them with lime.

Miss Penrod was stricken with the disease, and only Adelaide and Irene were left to take charge of the nightmare tasks.

Food was almost impossible to get. Vegetable stalls and butcher shops were closed because there was no one to run them. Thousands of the Japanese had been stricken. The bakery in the compound stood idle, for there was no one to operate it. Adelaide and Irene were almost in despair. By some miracle a huge box of Bovril arrived at the Rescue Home from Irene's brother-in-law in Ireland, and this essence of beef literally kept them going during the last days of the epidemic.

Somehow Irene and Adelaide survived without contracting the disease, but the ordeal had taken its toll. They were gaunt and hollow-eyed, completely exhausted. Irene, normally plump, was down to 80 pounds.

Forty-eight of the inmates had died. The Home seemed still and empty, with only a few inmates left. Miss Penrod had recovered, but she was weak and spent. No one had enough energy left to carry on.

Word came from the home office in London that Irene and Adelaide were to return home as soon as passage could be found for them. Traveling with them would be Clara Cuthbertson, whom Irene had met at Karuizawa her first year in Japan, and her small son Gordon.

During the war, German submarines had decimated the merchant marine of the Allied Powers, and few ships were available. The missionaries found it incredibly difficult but finally managed to get passage on the *Monteagle,* a rusty old tub that had done valiant service during the war. There had been no time to paint or refurbish her, and she scarcely looked seaworthy, but that seemed of little importance to Irene and the others. Thankfully they boarded the decrepit old steamer. Their destination was Vancouver.

4

A Vision at Sea

A sorry-looking little foursome stood on deck that day in August, 1920, watching the port of Yokohama disappear in the distance as the *Monteagle* chugged out to sea. The brown dress Irene wore was several sizes too big for her, and it hung in uncomplimentary folds about her body. Adelaide, always slender, seemed even taller and more angular. Her spectacles, perched on her aquiline nose, only partially hid the dark hollows under her eyes. Clara, who had worked in another area during the epidemic, was pale and thin; and even little Gordon showed the effects of the ordeal.

Yet their hearts were happy. Irene, who had relatives and friends in the States, was looking forward to seeing them. Adelaide was already dreaming of the green countryside of home. Clara, whose husband, Jim, had served in France during the war, was eager for the family reunion.

When the last glimpse of Yokohama had vanished, Irene sighed, "I feel as though I'm leaving the best part of my life behind me," she said.

"You'll be back," Adelaide said with conviction. But Irene was not so sure. She had planned to serve only two years. She had been in Japan nearly four. There was Al to think about. She thought of the little package tucked into her trunk, now down in the hold of the ship, and the two rings it contained. She had planned to return them to Al when she got home, but now suddenly as the homeward journey started, the thought of Al tugged at her heart. She would like a home and babies of her own. After the rigors of the past months, the dream was even more compelling. And she thought that there would be much rewarding work she could do as Al's wife—the wife of a minister—for he had graduated from the seminary now.

"I don't know," she said slowly to Adelaide." Maybe I won't be back."

"You're tired," her friend said crisply. "Don't try to decide now." Then, turning briskly in the businesslike way she had, she marshaled the little group down to their cabin.

They were traveling third class, and the cabin was small—minute might be a better word. Double bunks at each side of the room took up most of the space. Their hand luggage, piled in the middle of the floor, took up the rest. The room smelled musty and it certainly had not been refurbished for many a year.

"Well!" Irene chuckled, looking about. "The Lord isn't tempting us with worldly comforts on this trip!"

"I could sleep on the floor!" Adelaide groaned. And added ruefully, "If there were enough of it!"

"You'll sleep in an upper bunk," Irene decided. "And so will I. Clara and Gordon can have the lower ones."

They settled their cabin as best they could, and then went out to inspect their fellow passengers. They found a motley assortment—Orientals, brown-skinned and black people, a sprinkling of whites—all chattering and talking, and all as crowded in their quarters as the missionaries were.

"I do hope there's plenty to eat!" Irene said. "I can scarcely remember when we've had a square meal! Wouldn't it be wonderful," she added wistfully, "if there were roast beef for dinner?"

The hungry missionaries could not help looking forward to their first meal on the creaking vessel, but they were doomed to rude disappointment. Relegated to the third sitting, they found that the *Monteagle* provided little in the way of service. Tablecloths were soiled by the time they arrived. The galley was depleted. A watery kind of stew, its ingredients unrecognizable, was served to them.

"Well," Irene said, trying to be cheerful, "we Irish always say that stew, no matter what kind, is good and filling!"

She took a bite and her face changed. The stew, whatever it was, had obviously been made with tainted meat. It simply could not be eaten. Stoically Irene reached for a piece of bread and butter.

"It looks as though we're going to enjoy plenty of the staff of life on this trip," she said *sotto voce*. Then, as the faces of the others fell, she laughed merrily. "Oh, my!" she said. "I remember those sandwiches we used to make at Meath Place for the ragged children. Not a one without jam or meat! What I wouldn't give to have one in my pocket right now!"

As usual, Irene's good spirits restored the spirits of the

others, and they made their plain meal of bread and butter and tea cheerful in spite of the drawbacks.

Irene's mind was buzzing with plans. When the poor meal was over, she bustled away from the others, saying that she had something she wanted to see. Using her Irish charm, she inveigled her way to the first-class deck and before long had engaged a prosperous looking woman and her husband in conversation, and was recounting stories of the missionary work in Japan, with just a *little* mention of the conditions which existed for the third-class passengers in the dining room.

"The Lord helps those who help themselves," she said to herself, with a twinkle in her eyes. And if the truth were told, she was not surprised when, that very evening, a generous box of muscatel raisins and tins of biscuits arrived at their cabin.

"What have you been up to?" Adelaide asked suspiciously.

Irene chuckled. "The Lord's work!" she said.

Adelaide threw up her hands in mock despair, and Clara laughed. Little Gordon already had one tin of biscuits opened, and they all helped themselves. Nothing had ever tasted better.

After prayers, the little group prepared for bed. Irene and Adelaide went first while Clara and Gordon waited in the passage. Then when they crawled into their bunks, the others followed.

Finally they were all settled, and only the nightlight was burning dimly. Irene began one of the children's hymns softly, and the others joined in. As the last words died away, the friends said goodnight to each other and settled deeper under their covers.

Just as Irene was drifting toward sleep, she heard a scratching noise at the end of her berth. Her eyes flew open, and she lay perfectly still, staring toward the source of the sound. As she watched, she felt the hair at the back of her neck begin to stiffen. A rat poked its head from a hole in the bulkhead. Whiskers quivering, his beady little eyes seemed to search the cabin. Then, emerging from the hole, he marched across Irene's bunk, followed by another, and then another.

Irene heard Adelaide's sharply indrawn breath and knew she had seen what was happening. Then she heard Clara's frightened whimper and a small cry from Gordon.

"Hush!" she whispered. "Keep still and don't move!"

The rats skittered down from Irene's upper berth, scrambled across Gordon's below her while the child lay wide-eyed staring at them. Clara made a sharp sound, and Irene knew that she was ready to leap across the cabin to him.

"No!" she whispered sharply, and Clara was still.

The parading rats crossed Gordon's berth, scrambled to the floor, crossed the cabin, marched across Clara's bunk and up to Adelaide's. Then, one by one, the procession vanished through another hole.

Instantly the four occupants of the cabin were sliding from their bunks. Clara caught Gordon to her, shaking with fright. Adelaide, the spectacles she had retrieved from the bolted-down table perched on her nose, was looking militant. For a moment everything was in confusion.

"Wait, now!" Irene cried. "We're all losing our wits! The thing to do is to stop up the holes!"

There was not much to use—two missionary magazines, a copy of an English-language newspaper, and the wrappings from the tin of biscuits. The missionaries stuffed the holes as best they could, but they got little sleep that night.

The next day they reinforced their barricades with hand towels, but it was a tense group which lay, eyes wide open, in their bunks that night.

Promptly at the same moment that the rats had appeared the

night before, there was a scratching and scuffling. The rat family had a little trouble in dislodging the stuffings, but they managed. Once more they paraded along the same course, stopping on Adelaide's berth while the head rat worried the stuffing from the exit hole and Adelaide, her patrician face set in lines of horror and distaste, lay rigid.

The parade of rats became a nightly ritual. "Here they come, Mama!" Gordon would cry. Then the four human occupants would dive under the covers and the rats, now dubbed the Methodical Family, would march from the entrance hole through the cabin to the exit.

"Well," Irene sighed after their fourth attempt to stop the unwelcome visitors had failed, "I know they're God's creatures, but I never could understand why He invented them!"

"The big one's funny," Gordon, who with a small boy's adaptability had lost his fear of the famous rat family, said. "He's smart! I bet I could train him!"

The three ladies promptly squelched any such idea, and they continued to hide their heads and endure the nightly visitors as best they could, leaving Gordon to watch if he wanted to.

In spite of the rats and the inedible meals which forced them to exist largely on bread, butter and potatoes, the journey was not without its recompenses. Several times the friends Irene had made among the first-class passengers invited them to tea, and there were gifts of chocolate and powdered milk which were a godsend to the undernourished missionaries.

Irene also found that the journey gave her time for deep meditation. The experiences of her three and a half years of intensive work in Japan took on new meaning. Now with a little distance separating her from the strenuousness of the daily routine, things began to fall into proportion. She felt a sense of progress in her life and a continuing thread of developing understanding. The parts of her life were fitting together like a mosaic, and a picture seemed to be emerging.

One day in her reading she came across a verse in the Bible she had never noticed before. It was the Syriac Version of Proverbs 4:12, and it read: "As thou goest step by step, I will open up thy way before thee."

Irene read the verse several times, then sat looking into the distance. The words of the Scripture seemed to speak to her personally. She could not get them out of her mind. Somehow they seemed to have a special message for her.

Finally the sea voyage came to an end, and the *Monteagle* docked in Vancouver. The little group was met by the two Vernor sisters, JEB representatives, and taken to their beautiful home. The rooms were gracious, the appointments charming, the bed linen fine and clean. And Irene was never to forget the first dinner in the Vernors' home—the beautiful Irish linen tablecloths with a gloss on them from patient ironing, the sparkling silver and glassware. They were served British Columbia salmon that first night, with a garnish of salad; and when the meal was finished, Irene leaned back in her chair, her eyes almost misty.

"I almost feel like a pagan!" she said. "Do you think I'm backsliding?" Everyone laughed.

Clara Cuthbertson and Gordon left the same evening, anxious to get home. Irene and Adelaide stayed on as guests of the Vernors until they were rested amd restored to some measure of health. The guest room they occupied contained a lovely pen and ink sketch of a winter landscape. It pictured a cluster of leafless trees silhouetted against the snow-covered earth. Footsteps trailed across the snow. Under the picture was a Scripture text: "As thou goest step by step, I will open up thy way before thee."

Adelaide did not know that the verse had already made a deep impression on her friend. But she saw Irene studying it day after day.

"What is it, Irene?" she finally asked.

Irene whirled to her. "What's the Lord trying to show me?" she demanded almost fiercely. "Does He want me to go back to Japan?"

Adelaide grew quiet. "That is something I can't answer for you," she said.

"Oh, I know!" Irene burst out. "But it's *plaguing me,* Adelaide!"

She paced back and forth, all the innermost thoughts she had been keeping to herself pouring out. She talked of Al, and of the real love she had for him, and the dream of a home, and of the work there would be in Dublin at the Friends' Mission.

"It would be a *good* life!" she said tightly. "And very worthwhile, wouldn't it?"

"Are you trying to convince me or yourself?" Adelaide asked quietly.

"Oh, I don't know!" Irene cried, flinging herself down on the bed. "Adelaide, I don't know! I want to stay home! But something keeps pulling me back to Japan. You come from the 'Border country,' and you're more conservative than I am! Am I just being impulsive?"

"You must decide that for yourself," Adelaide said. "And prayer will help you."

"I know!" Irene said, jumping to her feet and beginning to pace again. "I *have* prayed, Adelaide. You don't *know* how I've prayed! But I can't seem to see the answer." She whirled to her friend. "That verse up there on the picture! Somehow I feel that my heart is being tried by it!" She stopped and stood still, looking at the picture with the Scripture line beneath it. And then she said more to herself than Adelaide: "I am willing to go where the Lord wants me to."

Suddenly her mind was filled with thoughts of the little children she had seen at the Rescue Home. She saw Shige San's face. She saw the little waifs and orphans, the children sold into vice. They seemed to be clustered around her, and she felt the tug of their small hands, saw the plea in their eyes.

She turned suddenly to Adelaide, her eyes intent, a look on her face that her friend had never seen.

"It would be better to put a fence at the top of the precipice," she said slowly, "than an ambulance at the bottom."

Adelaide sat quiet. This was not a time, she knew, to interrupt her friend's private thoughts. Irene's head was lifted, and her eyes were looking into the distance. She spoke without being aware that she was saying her thoughts out loud.

"We could save them!" she said. "We could save the little girls from the baby farms where they're taught to sing and dance and become future geishas. We could take little girls whose parents give them to evil men, thinking that they go to good lives. We could take the little unwanted ones and bring them to Christ!"

She walked slowly to the window and stood looking out. Adelaide remained silent, watching her friend. Without turning, Irene said low: "When the Lord is guiding your life, you can't go into Bypath Meadow. You have to go on straight for Him."

She turned and looked into Adelaide's face, and her friend met her look with the strong faith of her own spirit.

"I think I know what I must do," Irene said quietly.

Adelaide nodded, but asked no questions. "I'm sure the Lord will open the way before you."

Neither Irene nor Adelaide spoke again of what had transpired in that room, but there was a strong feeling between them, and somehow Irene felt that whatever her decision, Adelaide would be with her.

After several weeks in Vancouver, the young women left for home. They made a brief stop in New York to visit Irene's brother, Fred, and his family, and while there Irene was asked to speak at a meeting at Hephzibah House. She chose as her text the 16th verse from the 31st chapter of Proverbs: "She considereth a field and buyeth it." She did not know what made her choose that verse, for it really was not a particularly likely text for a lecture.

She spoke well that evening, describing the work in Japan—the Homes and the missions which were established there. Perhaps these were the fields.

When she had finished, a well-dressed woman from the audience came to speak to her. "What are you going to do when you return to Japan?" she asked.

For a long moment Irene hesitated. Then her eyes met the woman's, and she spoke simply and clearly: "I am going to establish a home for little girls," she said.

The woman's look deepened. She opened her purse and took out a bill, pressing it into Irene's hand. "Here is part of the price of your field," she said. "And may God bless you as you enter it."

She had given Irene twenty dollars. Looking at it, Irene's spirits soared. This, she was sure, was the Lord's confirmation that He wanted her to start a Home in Japan.

When she boarded the ship from New York to England with

Adelaide, the feeling of the Lord's confirmation was strong within her. Adelaide asked her no questions, but all the way across the Atlantic she could sense the new purpose of her friend. They landed at Birkenhead and went to London together, there to report jointly to the JEB council, and then go their separate ways.

When they were ushered before the Council, they were warmly welcomed by Barclay Buxton, who was in the chair. Paget Wilkes, the field director, sat next to him.

Adelaide gave her report first, and when she had finished, Mr. Buxton asked her if she had any particular work she wished to follow.

She shook her head. "No, I just want to be in evangelistic work," she answered.

Then Irene reported. A different question was posed to her at the conclusion of her report. "Do you feel that God is leading you to go back again?" the chairman of the Band asked her.

Irene sat a little straighter. She knew that the Band had a policy of engaging only in direct evangelistic work, and what she felt to be her call was outside of this realm. Yet this must not stop here.

"Yes, I do," she said firmly. "But under what board I do not know. I feel that I am not called to go back into the rescue mission or even to the regular work of the Band."

Surprise showed on the faces of the council members, and a murmur ran through the room. Irene was asked to explain. Speaking slowly at first, and then more surely, she unfolded her plan. Her words seemed to gather force; and as she spoke of erecting a fence at the top of the precipice, the room was very still.

"I want to save those children from being lured or sold into a life of vice!" she concluded passionately. "This I feel is my call!"

There was a moment of utter silence, and then an audible murmur of assent filled the room. Barclay Buxton rose and came around to her. He took her hand. "The Lord has given you this vision," he said, deeply moved. "You must go ahead."

There was talk then of how to implement the plan, how to find funds for the work that she would do. Money could not be diverted from the mission funds, but it was decided that Irene would continue as a missionary of the Band, and that any gifts received for her special work would be forwarded to her. She would also have their faith and prayer.

Irene left the meeting quietly exalted. She and Adelaide said their deeply felt farewells.

Irene headed for Dublin. There would be the members of her family to greet and to visit with, and to whom she must explain her new call. And there would be Al.

He was waiting for her at the pier, and his face showed all too well the joy he felt at Irene's return. He caught her hands in his, holding them tight, his eyes saying more than his words did.

"Welcome home, Irene! Welcome home!"

An overwhelming affection for him surged through her as they stood there holding hands that long moment, searching each other's faces. He had changed, of course—they both had. He was a man now, not a boy, and she saw the clean, strong lines of his face, the steadfastness in his eyes.

"It's *good* to see you!" she said in deep honesty.

"And you," he said, his voice rough with emotion.

Something within her would not permit her to let his hope be falsely nourished for even one more moment. She shook her head gently.

"I'm going back, Al," she said. "I'm only here on leave, and then I'm going back to the work in Japan which calls me. There's nothing more between us, dear friend. It is over for us."

Al's face whitened and pain showed in his eyes. His hands gripped Irene's so tightly that she almost cried out, but her steady gaze did not waver, and in it he saw all that was behind her words. Like Irene, Al was dedicated to Christian work, and no matter how it might personally hurt him, he could not question God's will. For a long moment he held her hands in his while his look searched her loved face. Then his hold on her relaxed, and his look gave her his blessing.

"God bless you," he said quietly. "You must follow His leading."

Tears stung her eyes, and he slipped his hand under her elbow and led her to the waiting buggy. She thought for a moment she was going to break down, and Al, knowing this, helped her. As they started off, he said the first thing that came into his head, though his voice was not quite steady.

"Do you remember how we used to go to school?" he asked. "In the donkey carts? And the only way we could make the beasts go was to dangle a carrot tied to a stick in front of their noses!"

They laughed shakily, and the moment passed. Al left her at the brick home in Mt. Pleasant Square where the family was waiting to be reunited with her.

There were happy times in the weeks that followed. Friends and relatives came from miles around, all eager to see Irene and hear about her experiences. She reveled in the family reunion, in the love and attention they gave her. Much as they would have liked to have her at home with them, none of them questioned her decision, and at night when she prayed alone in her room, she thanked God for such understanding and love.

As the weeks of her furlough slipped past, her mind was more and more occupied with the tasks ahead, and she prayed for guidance. One night at Liffeyview, she and Al took a long walk across the beautiful hills that surrounded her grandfather's old farm. She had brought the two rings, and she gave them to him now.

"The Lord *will* watch over us," she said softly, "though we are absent, one from another."

"I know," he said. "I have made my peace with the Lord and with myself. I know we must follow the steps which He has ordered." And then he told her that he had decided to enter a seminary in the states.

She looked up into his face. "Is it right for you, Al?" she asked intently.

"I think so," he said. "I feel this is where God is leading me." He was silent a moment, looking down at his hands. Then he looked back at Irene, his gaze straight on hers. "I'm not really letting you go," he said. "I am going to go on hoping. You have to know that."

"Even when I wish you wouldn't?" she asked, not really knowing what she wanted the answer to be.

"Yes," he said firmly. "Because I think we are meant for each other. I don't think it's someone else who is going to come between us. If it were, I'd have to let you go now, as you want me to. I think we are separating because the Lord's work comes first with each of us, and His word for us seems to be, 'Wait.'

And I will wait, Irene. I think you will, too."

"I can't promise," she said honestly. "I don't know how long this assignment may be, or where it may lead me next. I just know I don't want you to wait with false hope."

"If I wait," he said, "It will be my own decision."

"But I feel I'm holding you!" she whispered.

"I'm holding myself," he said. "And maybe for both of us. Don't try to make me change that!"

All the love Irene had for Al welled up in her; in her heart she hoped very much that when she had finished her active service to God, she might be allowed to come home to him. She put her hands in his, and they held tight to each other for a long, long moment. And then, using the strength and knowledge which was demanded of them, they said their final farewells.

Al took her home. They did not talk on that homeward stroll. They did not talk when they reached her home. They simply clasped hands again, and the feeling between them said all that mere words never could have.

Irene went into the house, and there she found waiting for her a letter from the JEB Home Council, directing her to return to Japan.

Below the letterhead there was a verse: "As thou goest step by step, I will open thy way before thee."

5

"*Get Thee South*"

On Decmber 21, 1921, almost exactly five years after her first arrival in Japan, Irene Webster-Smith disembarked at Kobe. A large group of JEB missionaries and workers were there to greet her, including Adelaide Soal who had preceded her to Japan. Then Irene was whisked away to the home of Paget Wilkes, now back at work in the field, where she would stay until her own work was started.

She was delighted to be back in Japan, and she couldn't get enough of walking about the streets, stopping to speak to the small shopkeepers, letting the *feel* of the country flow through her. She was inspired by the work which lay ahead, and this reunion with her adopted country seemed to make new strength flow through her veins.

There were meetings to attend, of course, and there were

pleasant social gatherings. One was a luncheon which Paget Wilkes gave for a noted Japanese gynecologist and obstetrician, Dr. Hezekiah Saiki and his lovely wife. The Saikis were Christians of long standing, and they were more than interested in Irene's plans to rescue little girls from lives of shame. They listened intently to all she had to say, and when she had finished, Dr. Saiki rose and came to her side. Bowing low, he took her hand.

"I am so glad you have come," he said. "But what a long time you have been in coming."

She looked at him in astonishment. "Whatever do you mean, Dr. Saiki?" she demanded.

He smiled down at her. "I have been praying for fifteen years that God would send a foreign missionary to do this very work," he said. And then he went on to explain that he and other doctors whom he knew felt that no Japanese woman could do it. "The government is too involved in the wretched system," he said. "So we asked God to send us a missionary."

"And here I am," Irene said, her eyes sparkling. "Very willing to accept any help that may come to me!"

Everyone laughed, and then, excusing himself, Dr. Saiki spoke earnestly with his wife a few moments. Then, beaming, he turned back to Irene.

"Perhaps we'll be the first to help," he said. He explained that he had just built two small houses in Kyoto behind their own home, intending them as an investment. "But I believe they are just what you need," he said. "The houses are duplicates. There are three rooms downstairs and two bedrooms upstairs in each. We want you to come and look at them. They are yours if you can use them."

Irene felt her spirits rise with joy, and then sink. She had already set her heart on starting the children's home in the Boshiu Peninsula, a verdant area within sight of Mount Fuji. In addition to being beautiful, it was one of the few places in Japan where one could find good pasture land, and practical Irene hoped to have goats and a cow to supply milk for the children who would eventually come to her.

She nearly opened her mouth to decline the offer, but she could practically hear Adelaide cautioning her not to be too hasty, and she swallowed the words.

"I'd be pleased to look at the houses," she said. "And I thank you from the bottom of my heart."

If there were reservations in her mind when she went the next day to visit the houses, she did not show it. She found the duplex attractive, and it would certainly give her a good start toward a Home. Still she couldn't bring herself to make a commitment. She had those green pastures of Boshiu in her mind!

In the next few days she and Adelaide visited a number of towns on the Boshiu Peninsula, and in each community they were told that they and the Home would be welcome. They were shown several available places which were certainly just what Irene wanted. Still she held back. She was experiencing what the Quakers call a "stop" in her mind.

Weary from her travels, and cross with herself because she could not come to a decision, she asked Adelaide to join her in prayer. "Lord, if you want me to go to Kyoto, make me *willing* to be *willing,*" Irene prayed. And added with typical honesty. "I really don't *want* to go!"

The prayer finished, Adelaide turned to the *Scripture Union* Bible portion for the day. One phrase fairly shouted at Irene:

"Get thee down south."

That was enough for both of them. Without more ado, Irene

accepted Dr. Saiki's offer, and went to Kyoto. "I had nothing more to say," she reports.

Only a year later the Boshiu Peninsula was one of the areas most damaged by fire and tidal waves in the great earthquake of 1923!

Irene started Sunrise Home in February, 1922, in Dr. Saiki's twin houses. To her delight, Adelaide Soal was assigned to work with her. Neither of them had any experience at all in setting up a children's home, but they set to work, letting their imaginations be their guide.

The orphanage was typically Japanese except for the western beds and some of the personal belongings of Irene and Adelaide. There were the *shoji,* the sliding paper screens which served as windows and walls. There was the *hibachi,* a huge glazed bowl which held live coals for cooking and boiling water for tea. In the center of the main room was the *kotatsu,* a hole in the floor in which wood or coal burned. Above this was a table over which a *futon,* or quilt, was thrown. Several children or adults could sit around the table with their feet tucked under it, the quilt held snugly around their waists.

Finally when the house was ready, they turned and looked at each other.

"What do you think?" Adelaide asked nervously.

"It *looks* fine," Irene said. And then, all too well aware of her own and Adelaide's lack of experience in caring for infants, she burst out: "But, please, Lord, don't send us anything less than a two-year-old!"

The next day the two friends went shopping for the few last items on their list, leaving Kageyama, their newly hired Japanese maid, in charge.

When they returned, they found her walking up and down in

front of the house, a squalling baby in her arms.

"Is that your baby?" Irene demanded, thinking that she had probably told them a fib about not being married so she could get the job.

She gave them a look. "No, it's yours!" she said. "The doctor-san brought him. It's mother is dying in the hospital, and the baby has done nothing but cry since it came here!"

"What have you done for her?" Irene asked indignantly.

"I have walked up and down with it on my back," she retorted. "Then I carried it in my arms. I tried to hush it. I tried to give it milk and it wouldn't take it. I'm sick of it. You can have it! I'm going to bed!"

She thrust the baby into Irene's arms and went stalking off. The two missionaries looked at each other. The baby wailed louder.

"Well," Irene said, "we'd better get started."

They carried the infant into the kitchen. Adelaide heated water while Irene unwrapped the pinch-faced little one. She couldn't suppress a gasp when she saw how thin and sickly the baby looked.

The missionaries put a washtub on the tatami floor and a towel in the bottom of it. Carefully testing the heat of the water, Adelaide filled the tub. Irene picked up the baby, which was only a few days old.

"Lord, don't let it fall to bits!" she prayed.

They lowered the infant girl into the warm water. The forlorn cries stopped. The tiny baby stretched out her little legs, soothed by the water. Carefully, they bathed her and then wrapped her in a clean towel. Adelaide heated a bottle of milk, and together they fed the infant which drank every drop. They took turns watching over the baby all of that night.

Dr. Saiki arrived early the next morning. "I have come to apologize," he said.

Irene's look twinkled at him. "You ought to!" she said with mock severity.

"I know you don't want children under two," the doctor admitted, "but this little one's mother is dying of cancer, and I thought the mother should have her few last days on earth free of worry. I told her you would take good care of her baby, and give her love."

Irene's heart filled with instant sympathy. "Of course!" she said. "We already love her."

The doctor asked Irene to go with him to the hospital to visit the mother, and she agreed readily. They bent over the thin, quiet woman who lay in the hospital bed.

"This is the lady our loving Lord sent to care for our little children," the doctor said. "She is happy to have your little one."

Irene nodded and smiled at her. She spoke with her gently, and the worry and tension left the woman's face. "Now I understand," she whispered, "what the doctor has been telling me about God's love."

She confessed her faith in Christ, and Irene prayed with her. Three days later, she died. The doctor offered to take the baby back to the hospital, but Irene wouldn't let him. "She's wound her way into my heart," she said. "She's our first child. We can't let her go."

Soberly the doctor told her that the child could not live, cautioning her that she and Adelaide must not let their hearts grow too involved.

"The Lord is training us," Irene said. "We must keep this small one."

The young missionaries gave the baby all the love and care they had, and it grieved them deeply when, three weeks later, the little one died. Irene thought of all the children who had worked and prayed so that Sunrise Home could be established. She thought of the difficult task of reporting to them that the first child placed in her care had not lived. Her grief deepened.

The task of taking the infant's body to the crematory fell to Irene, and she made the sad trip low in spirits, even doubting the call which she felt she had had. Wearily she returned to the Home. There she found Adelaide bouncing a bonny two-year-old on her knee! The second child to come to Sunrise Home had arrived! Irene's heart lifted. Surely, this was a sign that the Lord meant her to carry on.

The two-year-old was named Fusako, and she was a joyous, chubby little one who filled the Home with crows of delight. Irene's Irish heart was quickly lost to her, and she felt a deeper joy, for little Fusako had been unwanted by her parents, who felt that girl children were only a burden, and who had been willing to sell the child to a baby farm for a few yen. Dr. Saiki had learned of this, and had himself paid the price the parents wanted, and brought Fusako to the missionaries.

Her advent did not portend a procession of youngsters over two years old! This request of Irene's the Lord very apparently did not agree to! In short order, seven babies, all under a year old, arrived at Sunrise Home! But no one complained. Irene lined the babies in seven baskets along the floor and proceeded to care for them in assembly-line fashion.

"I'm learning a system!" Irene told Adelaide. "I start with the first one, bathe them right down the line, feed them in turn, and then change them! It's wonderful what a little organization will do!"

Irene wrote to Al: "We have a big, squarish pram—retrieved from the streets where it had been cast off!—and we give the babies their sunning in turn. It is wonderful, Al, how they respond to care and love! I can't help but feel that I am where I should be, though I confess I do miss you.

Al answered promptly, as he always did: "I know the Lord called you and you are where He wants you. I think of you and am proud of you. My work here goes well. I have a pastorate in New Jersey now, and the work is rewarding. I only hope that someday you will share this life with me."

"Oh, Adelaide!" Irene said when she read his letter. "Am I wrong in staying here? Should I be with him?"

"If you should be," Adelaide said, "you would be. But if you are questioning, keep asking the Lord to help you find the answers. He will guide you."

"I know," Irene said soberly. "I do ask Him, Adelaide."

Then, her smile cheerful, she went on with her work, chirping to each baby as she picked it up, giving each one an extra hug or a pat, loving them all very dearly.

One day when Dr. Saiki came to visit he looked very cross, although with typical Japanese politeness, he said nothing until Irene spoke.

"Is there something you would like to say to me?" she asked. "Are we doing something wrong?"

"Yes, you are!" he burst out. "You are loving those babies too much! You will break your hearts over them, because I doubt that you will be able to rear more than three out of seven! They've had poor starts in life. They just won't survive!"

Irene was badly shaken. It seemed incredible to her that so many of the children entrusted to her care must be doomed. She answered the doctor as best she could, and after he had gone, she wrote to her friends in Ireland and England asking them to pray for the babies in her care. She wrote fully about each child, giving their names so that each might be prayed for individually. Soon a host of Christians were carrying out the prayer injunctions, and it is possible to report that not a single one of the seven little girls died!

Sunrise Home was now teeming with activity. More children of various ages were being received, and Adelaide, whose heart had always been turned toward evangelism, had begun visiting neighborhood homes and witnessing for Christ. Sunday school classes were started at the mission. On Sunday evenings there were informal Bible classes for the professors and students from Kyoto University. On Tuesdays Adelaide held meetings for the women of the area. On Thursdays there were special classes for the wives of the professors. The little twin houses were busy as beehives.

Japanese women would drop in at any time of the day, curious and bright-eyed. They were forever asking how the missionaries dared to sleep on such high beds—weren't they afraid of rolling off them at night when they were asleep? They poked into cupboards to look at the Western style food, lingered over cups of tea to talk about spiritual matters. Many of them turned to Christ and sought instruction in their new-found faith.

Early in the second year at Kyoto, Irene—or Sensei as she was now widely called—took some of the most delicate of the children to the resort area of Mt. Heizan in the beautiful region above the city. The missionaries had a rough sort of shack there, and it was a delightful place.

While they were there, word came that one of their most needy little girls, Tomechan, had been stolen from the Home.

Irene rushed back to Kyoto. She searched everywhere she could think of, but without success. Then she reported the matter to the police.

"We can do nothing," they told her. "You have no legal right to the child."

The missionaries had taken Tomechan into the Home because she had become so sickly that her parents wanted to be rid of her. The child, who had been neglected and mistreated, was completely withdrawn. She looked at the missionaries solemnly, refusing to speak or smile. In the four years of her life, all she had ever known was to sit from morning until night assembling match boxes, which her father sold. Only when she had grown too ill to continue this slavery did her parents want to be rid of her.

The missionaries set about to nurse her back to health and to bring a smile to her lips. Her health improved slowly, but for many months she could not respond to love or happiness. Gradually, however, as she came to understand what caring and love meant, she learned how to be happy and romped and played with the other children. She particularly adored Sensei, who always had a special word or smile for her.

Sensei deduced that the parents had learned that Tomechan had grown well and strong again, and then they had stolen her from the Home so that they could once more exploit her. She set out to find the child.

They had moved from their previous home, and Irene could find no trace of them. The police would give her no help. She worried desperately over the little girl's fate.

The weather turned bitter cold, and the cold snap held the city in its grip for many days. Toward the end of this period, Irene had sad news from the police.

They had found little Tomechan. One night after her parents were asleep, she had slipped from the house and wandered about the streets, searching for the Home where she had found love. She wandered all that night and during the next day, sometimes asking passersby: "Where is Sensei?" If she had asked them for Smith Sensei, perhaps one of them might have been able to help her. But she was too young to know that name, and since every teacher and missionary in Japan was called "sensei," no one knew whom she meant. When she was finally picked up by the police as a lost child, she was ill from exposure. She died a few days later of pneumonia.

Irene determined that something must be done so that never again would any other little girl be taken from the Home as Tomechan had been. She sought out a Japanese lawyer who told her that there were only two ways to protect the children. Either Irene must become a Japanese citizen and include the children in her *seki,* or family registration . . . or the children could be adopted as British citizens.

Neither suggestion seemed suitable to Irene.

"Imagine!" she said to Adelaide. "Children being saddled with a name like Eiko-san or Yoshiko Webster-Smith! It's ridiculous!"

She continued to ponder the problem and to pray for wisdom. One day soon afterwards, a Japanese gentleman, Yamaguchi San, who worked with the JEB in Tokyo, came for a visit. As he was taking his departure, he said: "Now Sensei, if there is ever anything I can do to help you, please call on me."

On the spur of the moment, Irene asked him if he and his wife had children of their own.

"No," he replied. "God has not blessed us with children although we are very fond of them."

The idea sprang into Irene's head. "How would you like to be father to some of my children and have them put under your name?" she asked. He looked very nonplussed, and Irene explained her reason for asking this of him. She told him she would continue to provide and care for the children, and she asked him to discuss the matter with his wife when he returned to Tokyo.

It was not long before word came from Tokyo that the Yamaguchis would be delighted to have the children registered under their *seki*. Soon other Christian Japanese offered the use of their names, too, and there was no longer any anxiety about the children.

Sunrise Home continued to grow and thrive. With so many children it became essential to find larger quarters, and both Adelaide and Irene felt they would like to leave Kyoto and move to the town of Shin Maizuru, a naval port about three and a half hours away by train. Irene set out to find suitable quarters in that city, and she located an eight room house on the corner of the main street.

On October 25, 1924, the missionaries and their large brood and staff moved into the new-found location. They had not even had time to start unpacking before townspeople began to arrive, wanting to know when the missionaries were going to start conducting meetings!

"Not until we get unpacked at least!" Irene told them. Immediately several of the men pitched in, and in no time the Home was in readiness. That very night Adelaide conducted a gospel meeting.

There was great interest in Christianity. Meetings were always crowded. On Sunday mornings they had an average of 250 at Sunday school and had to conduct classes in relays.

Irene sent word to JEB headquarters that she thought an evangelistic campaign should be held, and a month later a veteran missionary came to conduct the tent meetings.

To the surprise of Irene and Adelaide, the municipal authorities suggested that the tent be pitched in the public park in the center of town. From the first night on the tent was filled to capacity, and people had to be turned away for lack of even standing room. By the end of ten days, 289 adults had professed conversion. The meetings continued for a month, and the evangelist thought that he must move on to other waiting communities, but the townspeople protested. They did not want him to leave. At last the tent had to be taken down in the middle of the night.

In less than a year, the new Home had already been outgrown. The gospel meetings Adelaide conducted nightly were so fully attended that two rooms had to be made into one, and seven of the children had to be put to bed in the dining room until the meetings were over, then carried, beds and all, back to their own room.

"Well," Sensei sighed to Adelaide, "I guess I must find another house. I'm beginning to feel like the Lord's real estate agent!"

The principal of a boy's school in nearby Maizuru suggested that they move there and that Sensei could teach a course in English at the school.

"If you'll find us a home, we'll be glad to come!" she told him.

In due time he called her to tell her that he had located what he felt sure would be suitable quarters. Sensei went to Maizuru, and she and the principal set out on foot to inspect the house. As they were walking, Sensei saw a beautiful pomegranate tree in full bloom and stopped to admire it. "Isn't it beautiful!" she exclaimed.

Her companion smiled. "Won't it be nice for you to look out on it every day?" he said.

Sensei looked at him in surprise. "But that's Count Makeno's property, isn't it?" she asked.

He nodded. "Yes," he said. "But it will be your garden." He told her that he had gone to Tokyo to obtain permission from the Department of Education for her to teach, and while there he asked if anyone knew of a place for her to live. Someone mentioned Count Makeno, the Controller of the Imperial Household, who spent eleven months of the year in Tokyo and might perhaps let Sunrise Home use part of his property. The principal called on him and told him of Sensei's work, and the Count and Countess gave their permission.

The house was a great, one-story rambling building with a little garden and a pool with a bridge over it. It had eight rooms downstairs, and Sensei saw at once that the attic could be partitioned off into three rooms where she and Adelaide could have a bedroom, study, and visitor's room. The work was begun immediately, and in April, 1925, Sunrise Home moved to these new quarters.

It was a happy location. There was a girls' school near-by which was convenient for the children. The gardens, which made a perfect playground for the children, were far more homey than their former location.

As in their previous quarters, Sunrise Home became a center for outreach. Adelaide was an indefatigable gospel worker, and the meetings she held were always well attended. Sensei conducted the Sunday school and did most of the managing of the Home, and in addition she taught English three hours a week at the high school. She was busy from morning till night, but the joy on the faces of the children and the knowledge that they were being saved from degrading lives made her work seem light.

It was not always easy going, however. Christianity and Buddhism were locked in a battle, and the work in the town was often difficult. Adelaide never halted her visitations, reaching out into twenty-two surrounding villages to contact women and children. Many received Christ.

One of the converts was Yamaji San, the eighteen-year-old daughter of a Buddhist priest. She arrived at Sunrise Home one evening, barefoot and wearing an old kimono. She had walked fifteen miles in the hot sun, and she told Sensei that after she had been converted, she felt she should be doing something for the Lord. She told her father she wanted to work at the Home, and he ordered her angrily from the house just as she was, without giving her a chance to take any of her clothing or personal belongings. She begged Sensei to let her stay at the Home where she would willingly do any kind of work there might be for her. Sensei gladly agreed, and Yamaji San became one of the Home's most devoted staff members

Little by little the family of "Sunbeams" was growing, and sometimes Sensei scarcely knew how she was going to manage to feed and clothe all the little ones. On one occasion the larder was empty. Even the last of the rice had been eaten for supper. "The Lord will supply what we need," Sensei told the children. "Let's pray now," the children clamored.

Early the next morning God put it into the heart of a local Japanese farmer from whom Sensei had once done a slight service to take a sack of rice and a huge basketful of fresh vegetables to the Home. Before this food was gone, unexpected funds arrived from England.

On another occasion, seven of the little girls came down with the whooping cough. They were kept in the upstairs rooms apart from the others, but the siege was a long one, and when they had all finally recovered, the doctor told Sensei that the children should be taken to the seaside for at least a week.

The children were delighted, but Sensei told them that she did not enough money for such an expensive trip. She suggested that the proposed trip be made a matter of prayer.

"I have to go to teach my English classes," she told them. "So you hold your own prayer meeting."

When she returned some time later, she found all seven of the little girls sitting on the stairs, one on each step; beside them seven little school bags crammed with doll clothes, skipping ropes, playthings and beads—but not a single comb or toothbrush or pair of pajamas! Sensei questioned them about their selection of items to be packed. They replied: "We know you'll take what we *need.* We're just taking what we *want!"* They were ready to go to the seashore and sure their prayers would be answered.

The next morning when the mail arrived, Hanako ran to get it. She came rushing back to Sensei, waving a letter and shouting: "It's come, Sensei! It's come!"

Sensei glanced at the postmark. It was Kent, England. "I'm sorry," she told the children who had gathered around her. "This letter is from someone I don't know. Our money comes through the JEB headquarters in Kobe."

"But, Sensei, we asked the Lord to send the money by the *first* post!" the children insisted.

Sensei tore open the letter. There was a note, and she read: "This afternoon I was in Tunbridge Wells visiting Mrs. Barclay Buxton, and I heard from her about your work with the children. I feel I must send you this gift now. I have a feeling it will arrive at a time of special need." Enclosed with the note was a check for twenty-five pounds. Sensei showed the money to the children, and seven little girls shouted with glee, seven little heads bowed in prayer as they thanked their Heavenly Father. They left next day for the seashore.

In 1926 Sensei left on furlough to spend time in England, the United States and Canada As she traveled from city to city, lecturing night after night, she always told her listeners how the Lord had led her step by step in her unique ministry. She made many new friends for Sunrise Home and her little "Sunbeams."

Her furlough over, Irene returned to Japan, and Adelaide, who had carried on while she was gone, left for her own well-earned rest. There were now many little girls in the Home, and each had her chores to do. The older children helped the younger ones to dress and comb their hair. They helped keep the house clean and tidy, and even the smallest ones learned to pick up their toys and games when they were finished with them.

Large as the house had seemed when they had first moved in, it was crowded now. And Sensei began to realize something else. The work at Sunrise Home had developed into two parallel activities. Caring for the children and leading them to full Christian lives was one. Adelaide's evangelistic work was another.

Sensei pondered this matter. She could not help feel that the two activities should be separate. But she thought of her dear friend Adelaide. They had been through so many things together and they had seen the blessing of God on their work. It would be difficult for them to be parted. Still, Sensei felt that the gospel meetings and adult Bible study classes were affecting the children. All too often just when the children wanted to let off steam at play, a study class or prayer meeting was in progress.

Sensei spent an entire night in prayer about the matter. As the first light of dawn crept through the window, she knew that she must write and tell Adelaide that she felt their work must be carried on from separate locations. She agonized over the letter, and after she had mailed it she wished she had not. She was afraid that Adelaide would be hurt, and she prayed that this might not be so.

Just a month later, a letter arrived from Adelaide. It expressed the very thoughts that had been in Sensei's mind. Their letters had crossed. On the very day that Adelaide received Sensei's letter in Carlisle, England, her message reached Sensei in Maizuru.

Two Bible verses rushed to Sensei's mind. The first was the fourth verse of the 95th Psalm: "In His hands are all the corners of the earth, and the strength of the hills is His also."

The second, Psalm 59:10, read: "My God, with His loving kindness, shall come to meet me at every corner."

Sensei's heart sang with praise.

6

Early Days at Akashi

Sunrise Home had been located in Maizuru for five years, and Sensei knew that she would hate to leave the lovely spot, but she also knew that the home there should remain for Adelaide, and that she must again find new quarters for her growing "family."

She had heard that the most healthful place "east of Suez" was the little city of Akashi, on the lovely Inland Sea, near Kobe. With characteristic faith, the Irish missionary headed for the town and the office of the mayor. She introduced herself and told him that she was looking for a home.

"We're Buddhists here," he answered bluntly. "We do not want missionaries here."

"I'm a missionary," Sensei answered, "but my immediate need is to find a place for my children."

"How many do you have?" he asked.

"Twenty-four," she said promptly.

His eyes popped open. "How many husbands have you had?" he asked.

Sensei laughed merrily, and explained about the children.

"Well," he said when she had finished, "if your work is welfare work, I think we might be interested. Yes, I think it will be quite all right for you to live here."

Sensei asked him if he knew where she might find a large house, and he called Kioka, his deputy, who happened also to be a real estate agent. The pair started off together in the pouring rain. Kioka carried an umbrella, the top of which, although he did not know it, was gaily decked with paper festoons from some recent holiday celebration. He carried it with great elegance, and Sensei did not tell him that pink and green balloons and streamers of paper were dripping from it.

They trudged from place to place, but each time they stopped at a house, Sensei shook her head. "It is not large enough," she said.

At last, Kioka, soaked to the skin and weary of trudging about the city, grew exasperated. "All right," he said. "I will show you a place! It will hold a hundred, *and* it's the last one I have to offer!"

Sensei didn't want a house that large, but she followed along. Kioka led her to a long, deserted building on the outskirts of the city. The location, overlooking the sea, was beautiful. The building, Kioka told her, had been a hospital, but had been abandoned three years before when the doctor who ran it was killed at a railroad crossing. The yard was neglected, and the rain gave the hospital an even more forsaken look, yet Sensei was immediately attracted to it.

"How much is it?" she asked.

"It's owned by a Buddhist priest," Kioka said. "He has been asking fifteen thousand yen."

Sensei shook her head. That was far too much. Tired and discouraged she traveled back to Maizuru. A few days later she received a letter from the mayor of Akashi, asking her to return to see him as he had information about the hospital building.

She returned the next day. The mayor took her to call on the Buddhist priest. They found him among his idols in a room reeking of incense. His greeting was friendly.

After they had exchanged the polite and formal conversation which the visit demanded, he said: "Kioka has told me about the work you are doing. I am interested. I have some wayward boys living in the temple and they are a handful. You have girls. They must be worse."

Sensei smiled. "They are younger," she said. And she explained about the work.

He nodded thoughtfully as he listened. It was impossible to tell what he was thinking. He was a very old man. His face looked as though it had been carved from old ivory, and his eyes were inscrutable.

"You know that I am asking fifteen thousand yen for the building," he said. "It is well worth it. There are twenty-three rooms."

Politely Sensei bowed. "I have great respect for your honorable building," she said. "And I am glad that it has so many illustrious rooms. But in my humble teachings I have no use for so many rooms."

His eyes narrowed a little. "It is possible the sum of fifteen thousand yen is a little high," he said tentatively.

Sensei bowed gravely again. "It is possible we could put the extra rooms to use," she said, continuing their oblique Japanese business transaction, "if it might be of service to you to relieve your mind of the worries of such an old building, and one so difficult to rent."

He sat back, folding his arms. "Perhaps, since your work is of such a charitable nature, I would like to give it to you for half the price, or seventy-five hundred yen."

"It is very gracious of you," Sensei said. "The work I carry on is very worthy."

Elation bubbled inside of Sensei, but her face remained as serene as his. With many expressions of thanks and gratitude, she thanked him and told him that she would have to confer with her superiors, and that she would let him know.

Now all she had to do was convince JEB officials that the deal she had made was a good one. Jim Cuthbertson, her old friend, was acting field director at the time, and he came to inspect Sensei's proposed purchase. Sensei had been delighted when she knew he was coming, because she thought he would be easier to convince than Paget Wilkes.

But Jim Cuthbertson was not easy to convince at all! He looked over the property, and he could find nothing good about it at all. He told Sensei that not only was the price high, but her running expenses would triple. He pointed out that the railroad tracks were nearby and said she would find them a constant annoyance. He said that the Home would be hard to keep clean and was too large anyway.

Finally Sensei, who had already met and vanquished the Buddhist owner, broke in on Jim's objections.

"Look here, Jim," she said. "I'd just like you to know that unless God has that place for me, and unless He is sending me here, I don't want it! We must find out what the Lord's will is before we make a decision!"

Jim gave her a dour look. "Try not to influence things *too* much," he said glumly.

The next day Irene was reading the thirty-fourth chapter of Ezekiel, dealing with the shepherds and their flocks. The whole portion seemed to convince her that God was confirming her interest in the property located on the hill above Akashi. "I will feed them in good pasture," she read, "and upon high mountains . . . They shall dwell *safely* . . . and *sleep* in the woods . . . and I will make them and the places round about my hill a blessing . . . there shall be showers of blessing. . . . They shall dwell safely, and none shall make them afraid. . . . Thus shall they know that I the Lord their God am with them."

Then and there Sensei's decision was made. She told the field director that she felt God had directed her, and he offered no more objections. The final details of the purchase were completed.

A few days later Sensei went to inspect her new property again. As she went along the lane toward the building, an old farmer stopped her and asked her if she had bought the property. She said that she had, and he shook his head disapprovingly.

"It's a fine building!" Sensei defended her property.

"But haven't you heard?" he asked. "The place is haunted. It is full of ghosts!" He looked toward the old hospital. "I can tell you, none of us around here would walk up that hill at night! I have my fields here, but I've let them go without proper care, for I won't work here in the evenings!" He pointed to some houses on the hill. "Do you see those? They are all vacant. No one will live here! The place is haunted!"

"Nonsense!" Sensei said stoutly.

"Ah, yes!" he insisted. "Let me tell you!" And he went on to recount that abortions, then illegal in Japan, had been performed in the hospital after the first doctor had been killed, and that many women had died. "Their ghosts walk the place," he said.

Sensei did not argue. Her immediate concern was to make the building habitable, and she listed alterations and repairs she wanted. A crew of carpenters was hired, and so that the work might be properly supervised, Sensei decided that she and Oka-san, her faithful matron, should move in, bringing the five youngest children so that there would not be too much work for the staff at Maizuru.

The little retinue arrived just at dusk. The power company had promised to have the electricity turned on, but there had been a slip somewhere and there were no lights. The place looked eerie. In the flickering candlelight the shadows in the room seemed to move. Irish Sensei thought of the old farmer's stories. She did not believe them, but she wondered how Oka-san would react. She finally decided that the best thing to do would be to make a pilgrimage through the whole building, praying in every room.

Oka-san was none too enthusiastic; but after a scanty supper the babies were put to bed, and she and Sensei began their long trek, each holding a candle, and with plenty of spares in their pockets.

"I'll recite Scripture, too," Sensei said. "Something like 'the blood of Jesus Christ, God's Son, cleanseth from all sin.' "

Bravely they climbed the creaking wooden stairs to the second floor. The candle flames twisted and turned, and sudden drafts made them grow dim as though some unseen breath were trying to extinguish them. The rooms were murky. The women's shadows danced grotesquely behind them.

"Fear hath torment," Sensei whispered to bolster their courage. They went from room to room, quoting Scripture and praying that the Lord would cast all evil from the Home, and that people would come to know Jesus Christ in every room.

It took two and a half hours to go through the whole building, even though Sensei admitted that she was rather inclined to hurry the prayers. With a sigh of relief they finally finished. "There!" Sensei said. "Now we're prepared to still the children's fears before they ever get started! They're bound to hear the ghost stories from other children, so as soon as they come here, I'll simply tell them the story and what we have done."

At last the main repair work on the building was completed, and the place was shining and bright. The rest of the children and staff moved from Maizuru, and they were delighted with the spacious new Home and the beautiful view and with the sea that stretched before them. Miss Mercy Coles, who had been a governess of the Buxton children, joined the staff as a teacher of Bible and music.

"This must be a place of light," Sensei said. "Did not the Saviour say, 'Ye are the light of the world'? And did He not say, 'A city that is set on a hill cannot be hid'? To give witness to His words, we must leave the windows undraped and light every room each night so that every one will be a beacon to all who see the home."

While the carpenters worked on the final details, Sensei and the children weeded the neglected garden and cut the grass. Roses were trained along the fence and new flowers planted. Soon vistors began to arrive, the mayor and his little daughter among the first. He wanted her to learn English, and Sensei gladly welcomed her to one of the classes.

A Sunday school was launched, and children from the community began to attend. More and more came, and their parents followed them. The gossip about ghosts faded from existence.

At last all the work was completed. The carpenters had been so stirred by what they had seen at Sunrise Home that nine of them made professions of faith in Christ, and Sensei felt that indeed the new Home was blessed.

The day for the dedication came. Many of the city officials were present. JEB missionaries came from other areas. Dozens of the people of the community came. The old Buddhist priest who had sold them the property could not attend, but he sent a beautiful crimson scroll, on which was inscribed:

"May the roof of your house be kindness,
May the eyes shine out love;
May the atmosphere be peace
And may the sounds heard therein be joy."

Sensei was deeply touched, and she wrote to her friend Adelaide. "God has so wonderfully answered the old priest's wish for us, which struck the same note as my prayers for the Home. The Lord has shone out of these windows, and He has given sounds of joy in the house, and let it shine in the children's faces. Often people who see them come to ask us to explain our secret of happiness, and we tell them about the Lord Jesus Christ."

Sensei taught the children that they must be very careful about their actions at school and in the community. If they behaved badly, she told them, they would not only bring disgrace to themselves and to Sunrise Home, but to the Name of Jesus Christ.

One day when the younger girls came home from Primary School, they rushed up to Sensei's study, as was their custom. Holding out their hands, one slightly cupped over the other in

Japanese fashion, they chanted: *"Osanji chodai,"* which meant "Honorable three o'clocks, please." Sensei went to her cupboard and got the afternoon treat of little cakes, and put one into each child's hands. She noticed that Fujiko was not with the others, and one of the little girls let it out that the missing youngster had been punished at school. They did not mean to be telling tales, but when Sensei questioned them, they told her that Fujiko's name had been written on the blackboard for misbehavior.

"Whatever did she do?" Sensei asked.

"Fuji will tell you herself," they answered.

At supper time, Fujiko came in late and sat as far as she could from Sensei. At evening prayers all the little girls gathered to sit in a circle, but again Fuji was late, and she sat down just inside the door. Sensei made an excuse to go into the next room for a book of Bible stories, and when she returned she sat down on Fuji's right. This meant that Fuji would be the last to say goodnight.

When the prayers were finished, the children in turn bowed before Sensei. *"O yasuminasai, Sensei,"* they said. "Goodnight."

After a hasty bow and a quick goodnight, Fuji was about to slip from the room, but Sensei stopped her.

"Tell me, Fujiko," she said, "have you been a perfectly good child today?"

Fuji hung her head and gave no answer.

"Why don't you answer, Fujiko?" Sensei asked.

"I don't know how to tell you, the child admitted. Her eyes met Sensei's. "The teacher was unkind!" she blurted. "She called me an orphan! Am I? Am I not your child?"

"Of course you are my little girl," Sensei said. "Because I love you in my heart."

Fuji gulped and tears threatened. "I was bad!" she whispered. "I stuck out my tongue at the teacher when she wasn't looking, only she turned around and caught me. She wrote my name on the blackboard in big letters and made me stand under them, so everyone would know I was in disgrace."

"Whatever made you stick your tongue out?" Sensei asked.

"I guess it must have been the Devil!" Fujiko declared. "This morning when the bell rang, I stayed in bed and didn't take time to pray. The Devil has been bossing me around all day, and I'm just sick of him!"

Sensei suppressed a smile and asked Fuji if she thought the Devil was gone now, and the child nodded vigorously.

"You had better be sure and say your prayers tonight before you get into bed," she said. Then with a hug that told Fuji she was forgiven, Sensei sent her on her way.

There was something infectious about the joy in Sunrise Home. People began to move into the deserted houses on the hill, and the cluster of homes soon became a Christian parish. Mercy Coles' Bible classes were always filled, and she gave piano lessons to many of the children in the community as well as to the little "Sunbeams."

One evening the "family" was gathered in the front room, singing gospel songs as Mercy played. Sensei sat with her back to the window, a baby on either side of her, and she sang lustily with the children.

"Into my heart, Into my heart,
Come into my heart, Lord Jesus.
Come in today, Come in to stay,
Come into my heart, Lord Jesus."

One of the older girls signaled to her suddenly that someone was looking in the window. Sensei turned and saw an elderly man and woman peering into the room. She went to the door and invited them in. They apologized for looking in the window, but the woman said hesitatingly, "We heard such lovely singing, we wondered what sort of a place this was."

Sensei noticed that the couple were dressed in their best clothing, black kimonos with crests on their sleeves and back, and that they seemed to be troubled. She asked them to be seated and had the children sing several more songs for them. Then she repeated some of the messages she had given for the Shining Hour, which was what she had named the evening prayers.

"If we let the Lord Jesus come to live in our hearts," she said, speaking to the children but actually for the old couple, "the first thing He does is cleanse us from all sin. He will cast out all that is wrong, and He brings light and life and peace and joy to us."

Then the children prayed, starting with the small ones and working straight up the ladder of ages.

"Thank you, Jesus, for sending us visitors," one toddler prayed.

"Please send them back," another said.

"May they let the Lord Jesus come into their hearts," a third child prayed.

When all had finished, the whole "family" recited the Lord's prayer, and then the children, with Mercy Coles and Oka-san in charge, scampered off to bed.

Sensei invited the elderly couple to her sitting room for conversation and refreshment, but they said they had business to attend to and must be on their way. Inviting them to come again whenever they liked, Sensei said goodnight, and the old people went on their way.

After finishing her work, Sensei went up to bed. She had been asleep for some time when something woke her. Listening, she heard the sound of wooden clogs on the cement walk out front. She looked at the illuminated dial on her watch. It was 2:30 in the morning.

Quickly slipping from bed, she went to the window. "Who's there?" she called softly so as not to waken Mercy.

"The people who visited you this evening," the old man called back in a low tone. "May we come in, please?"

Pulling on her dressing gown, Sensei hurried to let them in. She took them into the dining room and brought tea for them. Little by little their story came out.

They had come by train from Osaka to Akashi. "We had a special purpose for coming," the old man said, his voice not quite steady. And he went on: "You know that these have been days of depression and hardship for many Japanese people. I am a worker in bamboo . . . I have always made beautiful things . . ."

His voice trailed off, and Sensei waited until he was able to go on. "I have made many beautifully carved pieces, but now there is no market for them. My trade has failed. We had come to the end of our resources. We decided," he said, "to take our lives tonight."

Sensei's heart skipped a beat, but she nodded to the man encouragingly. After another pause, he said: "We dressed in our best clothing, and came here by train. We planned to throw ourselves from the cliff to the railroad tracks below when the express train came along."

He was silent for a long time. Then he said: "When we left here, we went to the cliff and we tied our wrists together. But we could not jump. Something seemed to hold us, and we decided that it was the hands of your children. The sound of the singing and their prayers were in our ears, and we decided at last we must come back here for help."

Gently, Sensei talked to them, introducing them to Jesus Christ. Then she arranged places for them to sleep. Mercy was awake when Sensei returned to her room, and in low tones Sensei told her what had happened.

"Thank God they saw our light and heard the singing," Mercy whispered, and Sensei nodded soberly.

In the morning she escorted the old couple down to breakfast. The children were delighted, and chattered all through the meal. After the older ones had run off to school, the old man said that he had noticed that some of the children's chopsticks looked shabby. "If you will get some bamboo, I will make new ones."

Sensei sent Oka-san hurrying for the bamboo, and the old man spent the whole day making the new chopsticks. On each pair he carved "God is love," and added red coloring to make the letters stand out.

In her own mind, Sensei had already decided that the old people must stay on at Sunrise Home for she could not cast them aside. "They can live in the little house in the back of the Home," she told Mercy. "And they will both be useful. The old man can work in the yard and do little repair jobs around the house—we've been needing someone. His wife can help with the sewing and mending."

"There's always plenty of that!" Mercy laughed. "I think it's a wonderful plan."

So it was settled. When Sensei told the old couple, tears of joy and gratitude came to their eyes, and they could not thank her enough.

"Don't thank me," Sensei smiled. "It is the Lord Jesus who has brought all this to pass."

A few days after the old couple were settled, Sensei went to

Kobe to visit with Adelaide and some of the other missionaries who were in the city to confer with Paget Wilkes, who had resumed his duties as field director. She hadn't seen Adelaide for some time, and the two friends had a happy reunion. Adelaide was as full of zeal and energy as ever, but she admitted that it was sometimes hard going at Maizuru. Irene gave her all the news from Sunrise Home, and they exchanged news from various friends in England.

That evening, with two other friends, they attended services at the mission. The meeting ran late, and afterwards as the four women walked along a narrow, poorly lighted street on their way home, Sensei noticed a man standing on a corner. He seemed to study her closely.

"I don't like the looks of that man," she said to Adelaide.

The other two were a little ahead, and Sensei called out to them in Japanese so that the man would know there were four in the party.

They turned into a narrow lane leading up a hill. Deep gullies made by flood waters that ran off the hills during the rainy season bordered the road, and a huge stone wall stood just behind them. There were no houses here, and the women were nervous.

They could not see what had happened to the man, however, and Sensei tried to tell herself that she had probably only imagined that he looked at her so closely.

Then just as they rounded a bend in the road, the man leaped from behind a telephone pole straight at Sensei, knocking her down. Her foot caught in the gully, and her head struck the stone wall, dazing her. The man tried to wrest her purse from her, but it had a shoulder strap, and he could not get it away. The screams of the others sent him fleeing.

Sensei was dizzy and in pain. The others helped her back to the missionary house where they were staying and got her into bed. Adelaide wanted to call a doctor, but Sensei wouldn't let her.

"I'll be fine after a night's rest," she insisted.

But she was not. When she woke, she thought it must still be night, but she heard Adelaide moving about the room, and when Sensei stirred, Adelaide called good morning and asked how she felt.

Panic swept over Sensei. She sat bolt upright, turning her head from side to side in a vain effort to dispel the darkness. She half cried out, and Adelaide ran to her side.

"Irene!" she gasped. "What is it? What's the matter?"

Irene groped for Adelaide's hand and clung to it. "I can't see! she whispered. "Adelaide, am I going blind?"

Shock showed in Adelaide's face, and hastily she escorted Sensei to an eye specialist. He ordered her to enter the hospital. There were days of tests, and at last the doctor told her that the retina in her right eye had been detached, and the muscles in the other eye injured.

He held out little hope to Sensei. "The most seriously injured eye will not recover its sight," he told her gravely. "We can only hope that we may save the sight in the other."

Gradually most of the sight returned to her other eye. She was given a set of rules to follow—never to go out at night without a flashlight to guide her feet, never to carry heavy baggage or bundles, not to stoop, not to lift heavy furniture—a list which Sensei was soon to ignore.

Her furlough time was near, and the home office gave her permission to leave early for London. Al wrote urgently asking her to vacation in New Jersey, his letter showing his deep concern for her. She wrote back, reassuring him, and saying that she felt it best to go straight to London, there to consult a famous doctor on Harley Street. But after her visit to that doctor, she had little of good news to write to Al. The doctor could only confirm what she had already been told: Sight would never return to the one eye; it would never be good in the other.

Four doctors urged Irene to retire, and so did Al who hoped she would now at last come to New Jersey and become his wife. But Sensei thought of the children back at Sunrise Home, of the difficulties she had faced before, of all the work there was yet to do in the new venture of faith at Akashi.

And she thought of the verse which, so many years before, had been an inspiration to her: "As thou goest step by step, I will open up thy way before thee."

She had always trusted in that verse. She had gone step by step, and the way had been opened. Now in this new step of faith she was sure the promise given her so long ago would still be fulfilled.

7

The Conversion of Kazue

The Board did prevail on Irene to take a year's furlough, but if they had thought this would be a time of rest for her, they were badly mistaken! Wherever Sensei was she continued in service. Her whole life was ordered by the Lord.

She went first to Dublin to visit family and friends. Al, of course, was not there, and many others she had known were gone, but Irene found great joy in reunion with those of her family who remained, and in renewing old acquaintances.

She had only been there two days when she was called on to speak to the ladies of the Friends Sewing Circle, and she talked glowingly of the work at Sunrise Home and the little girls who lived there. Sunday she went to Friends meeting. One of the prim Quaker ladies who had been at the Sewing Circle, greeted her with considerable reserve.

"The stories you tell are very colorful," she said disapprovingly. "But I cannot help feel that you have a rather vivid imagination, especially where children are concerned."

The comment stung, and Irene's cheeks flushed. As she took her place in the pew, she hoped the Lord would not give her anything to say that morning. But as she sat meditating, she felt called on to speak, and she rose and gave a short message. It concluded with the words: *"A little child shall lead them."*

When she sat down, she noticed a mother near-by with little girls on either side of her. The lady was bending down to the youngest one, very evidently trying to dissuade her from something. But the child was determined. In an audible whisper, she said, "But Mummy I *must* sing, I *must* sing." She stood on the hassock between the pews and, gripping the seat in front of her, began to sing in a sweet little voice:

> "Jesus bids us shine first of all for Him;
> Well He sees and knows it when our light is dim.
> He looks down from Heaven to see us shine,
> You in your small corner and I in mine."

Finished, she sat down primly and folded her hands like any old Friend. There were some looks of disapproval, but many of the congregation were touched, for such a thing had never happened in meeting before.

When the service was ended, Sensei bent down and kissed the little girl. As she left the chapel, the woman who had spoken so sharply to her stopped her. "I must tell you," she said, "The Lord spoke to me when you talked at the Sewing Circle, and He spoke to me today when you stood up in Meeting, but my heart would not hear Him. Then that dear child sang, exactly as you had reminded us that a little child shall lead us."

She paused to wipe the tears from her eyes. Then she went on: "When I first came to Dublin, I was a bright Christian. But down through the years my light has grown dim. I have been praying, 'Lord, restore unto me the joy of my salvation.' When the child sang, I came back to the Lord."

Irene pressed her hand warmly, a prayer of gladness in her heart. Two weeks later, she learned that the woman had died. Her husband and sons told Sensei that the last days of her life were full of joy and happiness. Their whole home seemed to be flooded with light in the final days of her life.

Her visit in Dublin ended, Sensei set out on a long and busy speaking tour, not only in the British Isles but in Canada and the United States. Always adaptable in any country, she could speak to a drawing room gathering with the same aplomb as when she met with simpler friends in cottage meetings or mission halls. Everywhere she went she won new support for Sunrise Home.

Irene had hoped for at least a little time to visit with Al. She longed to see him and to know first hand of the work he was doing. But the rigors of her schedule gave her little time for herself. She did not even get to go to New Jersey to see his church and his parish. Instead he came to New York for a brief reunion with her, and they tried in the few hours they had to fill each other in on all the events of their lives and bridge the distance between them.

"I should write you more often!" Sensei said contritely, knowing she wished that they might be closer.

"I read your letters over and over," he answered. "They're—

very precious to me." He searched her face. "Is your work in the field nearing an end?" he asked. "Is our time any nearer?"

She shook her head slowly. "The Lord has given me no sign of when my work may be finished," she said. "And I must go on until He releases me. Do you understand, dear friend?"

He nodded. "If the time comes when you are released, you will tell me, Irene, won't you?" he asked.

"I will tell you," she answered. "You will be—the first to know."

At the end of her strenuous furlough, she returned to London for a brief stay at a rest home there. A letter was waiting for her, signed by twelve of her "Sunbeams."

"If anyone should offer you a piano," one paragraph said, "please do not say 'no thank you.' The one we have will not play any more, and we have been praying for a new one."

Sensei chuckled. A piano was rather a large order, she thought, and not a gift that any one was apt to give. On the present budget they certainly could not afford a new one. She tucked the letter into her pocket and went on about her business.

That evening when the gong sounded for supper, she went down to the dining room and was seated next to a woman she had met on a previous visit to London. The woman had lived in her own home then, but ill health had made it impossible for her to continue living alone, and she had moved to the rest home where she was happy.

She and Irene chatted pleasantly during the meal, and when it was over, the woman said: "Something you said at family prayers has been a blessing to me, and I want to show my thanks to God by sending a gift to your Home. While I was praying this afternoon about this, I was suddenly reminded of my piano, which is in storage. I'm going to sell it and give the money to you."

Irene felt her heart quicken. Without a word she took the letter from her pocket and passed it to the woman, who took it curiously. As she read, her face grew radiant.

"How wonderful!" she cried. "Of course you may have my precious piano for your dear girls. How lovely it will be to think of them playing it!"

"There's no end to what faith does!" Irene said intensely. Then she chuckled. "I must be sure to keep my own strong so we can get that piano back to Japan. The transportation costs are going to be formidable!"

The woman immediately offered some tithe money to help with the cost, and the next day Irene bustled off to see the Japanese shipping company which from time to time had transported bundles of clothing for the children at Sunrise Home free of charge. She had no hope that they would take anything as large as a piano but she did hope they might make a special fee for her, and she suggested this to the officials. To her amazement, they said there would be no charge at all!

The piano was crated and hoisted aboard a freighter. Irene, traveling by speedier liner, reached Japan first, where she was joyously greeted by the children and the staff. She kept the news about the piano a secret, for she wanted it to be a surprise. She couldn't help notice the bit of disappointment in Mercy Coles' face, for Mercy loved teaching the children, and piano lessons had been one way of also reaching the children of the community.

Eventually word come to Sensei from the steamship company

that the piano had arrived and was in the Custom House waiting payment of duty.

Irene went to the city the next day. When she reached the Custom House, she asked to see the chief official. "He doesn't see ordinary people," she was told.

"Perhaps you should ask him," Sensei said crisply, and the clerk went off, grumbling under his breath.

He was back in minutes, much more polite. The chief would see her.

Well aware of Oriental indirectness, Sensei spoke about the pleasant weather and inquired about the health of his family. Then she thanked him for the many favors he had shown to the Home in the past. He replied politely: "A piano is different. It is a luxury."

"I'm quite prepared to pay the duty," Sensei told him primly.

The chief did not seem in a hurry to take her money. He asked her if she had a piano of her own in Ireland. It seemed a strange question, but Sensei said that she had.

The chief pursed his lips and looked at her through his polished spectacles. "Well," he said at last, "if a piano is a regular item in your home, it is not a luxury for you." The piano, he told her, could come in duty free. Irene did not dispute his logic.

When the gift reached the Home, the children and Mercy Coles were jubilant. Sensei told them who had sent the piano, and the little girls promptly wrote her a thank you note. When she wrote to Sensei later, she said: "You cannot imagine how much joy this has brought me. Truly the Lord works in marvelous ways."

Life at Sunrise Home went on in its full, rich fashion. The climate was delightful. An abundance of fresh fruit and vegetables was always available. The children made many friends in school, and through them Sensei and Mercy came to know their parents. Many were converted, including the daughter of the Mayor of Akashi, and later the Mayor himself.

It was through him that Sensei came to know a beautiful young woman named Kazue Miki, the nineteen-year-old daughter of the president of the Osaka Stock Exchange who had a magnificent home on the seashore at Akashi. Kazue was a graduate of an exclusive girls school where she had learned to sew, make flower arrangements, and conduct the tea ceremony.

The Mikis were wealthy Buddhists, and before her contact with Sunrise Home, Kazue had been only interested in her beautiful clothing and the pleasures of her life. But from the first she was interested in the Bible classes, and she soon brought her younger sisters, both of high school age; and in time her younger brothers also joined the classes.

One day after Kazue had been coming to classes for about four months, she asked Sensei if she could spare her a little time that morning. Of course Sensei could, and she took the young girl up to her sitting room.

"Now," she said when they were settled, "what is it, Kazue?"

"You know that before I started coming here, I was completely taken up with worldly things," Kazue began. "There isn't anything my mother and father wouldn't buy for me, but since I've been attending your classes, I've lost my desire for worldly things. Instead I have a great desire in my heart for something spiritual. I believe it is the salvation of the Lord Jesus Christ that I long for."

Sensei talked with her for a long time. Finally she said quietly: "Would you like to accept this gift of salvation now?"

Without hesitation, Kazue said: "Yes, I would."

Sensei turned to the sixteenth chapter of Acts, and said, "Here is a beautiful verse that contains a question and an answer: 'What must I do to be saved?' and 'Believe on the Lord Jesus Christ and thou shalt be saved, and thy house.' Will you believe on him?"

"Yes," Kazue said earnestly. "I want to believe."

Together they knelt. First Sensei prayed. Then Kazue spoke to the Lord. She asked simply that He would cleanse her from all sin and would make her His child, and she said that she wanted to follow Him.

Sensei then prayed again, asking God to make Kazue a good witness. "Let her tell from a full heart what Jesus Christ has done for her today," she finished.

When they rose from their knees, Sensei said: "When you go home today, Kazue, will you tell your family what the Lord Jesus Christ has done for you today?"

Kazue promised. Later she told Sensei what happened that evening. When she arrived home, the family was already seated on the floor about the low table on which their dinner was served. They commented on her late arrival.

"I will tell you about it after dinner," she said.

After they had finished the fruit course, she turned to her father and mother. "I would like to tell you now what happened to me today," she said. "Do you mind if the servants come in?"

They said that they did not, and the servants were summoned. They stood quietly as Kazue spoke.

"I want you to know," she began, "that I am different from the girl who left this house this morning. I am a new creation in

Christ Jesus, and the Lord has forgiven my sins. I am ashamed that I have been such a selfish daughter and selfish sister, but I expect now to be different."

The beautiful girl told them of receiving Jesus Christ, and she concluded, her eyes shining: "The best thing of all is that you are all going to be saved. Every one of you. We are all going to be in this together."

There was silence when she finished, and even polite disdain on her father's face. But Kazue's conviction did not change. "You will see," she said.

That night Kazue began her work as a soul winner. It was her governess she first spoke to, for she had already noticed interest in the woman's face. The next morning she appeared at Sunrise Home with the older woman.

"This is Mrs. Shimauchi, our governess," she told Sensei. "She wants to talk with you. I'll play with the children in the yard while you have your visit."

As Sensei went to the door with her, Kazue whispered: "Be sure to bring her to Christ today."

That was quite an order. It was not easy to talk to a complete stranger about spiritual matters, and Sensei did not know quite how to begin. But Mrs. Shimauchi did not wait for her to start. She herself opened the conversation. "You know I am a Buddhist," she said. "My family are all Buddhists, *and I always will be a Buddhist,* but I want what Kazue found here yesterday. May I have it?"

"How much do you know?" Sensei asked. "Have you ever been to church or Sunday school?"

The woman shook her head. "But as you know," she said, "Kazue is preparing for the marriage her father has arranged for her. He is a Christian boy, and very polite. After breakfast each day the women of the house sit around and sew for Kazue. Actually, Kazue has not been doing much sewing. She leaves that to us while she tells us what you have taught her. She brings her Bible, and she explains each time what you have taught in your classes. This has gone on for some time, so you see, I know a little. I know enough to know that I need this Jesus Christ whom Kazue has enshrined in her heart."

After more talk and prayers, the governess accepted Christ. Kazue had won her first soul.

Day by day after that, Kazue sought to bring other members of the family and staff to Christ. She ticked off the names of her family to Sensei:

"Shimpei will accept Christ because he comes to the Bible classes. Toshiko is the same—he'll become a Christian. Juro doesn't come to classes, but he will. Masako is different—she is so taken up with sports she thinks of nothing else. Saburo is the youngest, still a boy. My mother is interested. But it is my father who is going to be very difficult. Still, I'm encouraged by what you said Sunday: 'There is no one too hard for the Lord!' I am clinging to that."

One by one the family members came, Shimpei first, then Toshiko, then Jiro, then Kazue's mother. Masako came to a few Bible classes, but then stayed away. One Sunday she turned up unexpectedly for Sunday school. Sensei was talking about the Commandment: "Remember the Sabbath day to keep it holy," a teaching which the Buddhists, of course, did not follow.

"There is only one thing to do about this individually," Sensei told her class. "Instead of regarding Sunday as your own, you must think of giving your Sabbaths to the Lord."

Masako stayed after the lesson. "I've decided," she told

Sensei. "I'm going to give my Sabbaths to the Lord. I have been very unhappy—staying away from classes, and feeling so far away from my brothers and sister."

She looked up at Sensei. "I was elected captain of my netball team," she said. "It was something I wanted very much. But now I don't want it. I'm going to resign, because all of the games are played on Sunday, and I want my Sundays as presents for the Lord."

She accepted Christ a few days later. At this time the Miki children asked their parents if they could hold Christian meetings in the family home so they could invite their high school and college friends. Permission was given.

The lovely home contained three front rooms. As a Japanese would describe their size, the first was a twelve-mat room, the second a ten, and the third an eight. By removing the beautifully decorated shoji between them, one huge room was formed.

Soon the great room was filled at every meeting. Friends and relatives joined the young people, and often Sensei conducted the meetings. Mr. Miki never attended, but Sensei noticed that the shoji separating his study from the room where the group met was usually ajar. After the meetings, he often joined the others for refreshments, and he always urged the young people to come again.

In time all the family and staff had accepted Christ except Mr. Miki. He hinted once to Sensei that there were problems which held him back, but he did not say more.

About this time, Sensei heard that Paget Wilkes would be visiting the Home. "What a grand opportunity to invite Mr. Miki to dine with Mr. Wilkes, and then leave them to talk together after dinner," she told Mercy Coles.

Mercy smiled. "If there's an opportunity in sight," she said, "I know you will seize it."

Sensei did. When Mr. Wilkes arrived, she sent an invitation to Mr. Miki who accepted promptly. On the night of the dinner, things went as she had planned except when she tried to slip away to leave them alone, Mr. Miki asked her to remain.

"Since you have led my family to Christ," he said, "I want you to hear what I have to say."

Sensei took her knitting and sat quietly while Paget Wilkes pressed the claims of Christ upon the wealthy Japanese. Finally Wilkes asked in a paraphrase of a Bible verse: "What doth hinder you to come to Christ?"

Mr. Miki did not evade the question. He answered in the crisp, orderly words of a businessman.

"There are three reasons. First, I am the head of my family (he referred not only to his immediate family but the entire clan relationship). Many of them remain Buddhists. It is my duty to see that the shrines are cared for and that offerings are made each day. If I became a Christian, I would fail in this responsibility.

"Next," he said, ticking his second reason off on his fingers, "I am the president of the Osaka Stock Exchange. I have been on the Exchange since I was eighteen. I would have to give all this up if I became a true Christian, for a Christian must be honest, and I am afraid that some of the deals in which I am involved are not.

"There is one more thing," he said, looking at Sensei. "As you know, my business is in Osaka. Instead of returning home each night, I remain in Osaka Monday, Wednesday, and Friday nights. My family thinks I stay in a hotel, but I do not. I have another house in Osaka, and a beautiful mistress. She was a geisha of all geishas, and now she is mine. If I become a Christian, I will have to give her up."

Sensei interrupted the conversation for the first time. "May I ask just one question?" she said. "Do you have any desire to become a Christian?"

Mr. Miki nodded. "I have every desire," he said. "When I see how happy the members of my family are since they have found Christ, I have *every* desire. But what can I do?"

"You must be born again," she said, and went on to remind him that accepting Christianity is a spiritual birth. "When you really belong to the Lord," she said, "He begins to undertake for your every need. In every emergency that arises, you can count on Him."

Mr. Miki nodded but did not speak. Sensei went on speaking: "To those who receive Him, that is, the Lord Jesus Christ," she said with a quotation from the Gospel of John "To *them* gave He power to become the sons of God. He will undertake for these difficulties and hindrances once you have committed your life to Him." She paused for a moment, and silence filled the room. Sensei leaned toward Mr. Miki. "Will you accept the salvation of Christ?" she asked.

Tears filled Mr. Miki's eyes, and he began to pour out his heart in prayer to the Lord. That night he came to Christ.

Some weeks later a message came to Sensei saying that Mr. Miki would like to see her at their home. She hastened to go there, and she was greeted by her host.

"I have asked you to come," he said, "because today we are going to burn our idols. We all wanted you to be here."

The shrine, a beautiful black lacquer cabinet, had already been broken up and the pieces removed to the grounds and placed in a basinlike concrete structure which normally held water for protection against fires.

The family and staff gathered around. Mr. Miki spoke: "If any of you have anything that has hindered your growth as a

Christian, now is the time to get rid of it," he said.

One by one the family and staff members brought their 'hindrances' and tossed them on the heap. Gods and idols were piled there. Worldly possessions which might be temptations were added.

"This house is now dedicated to the Lord," Mr. Miki said, and ignited the pile. The flames leaped into the air. The family and servants stood with Sensei, holding hands and singing in Japanese:

> "To God be the glory,
> Great things He hath done.
> So loved He the world
> That He gave us His Son."

The Miki's always a compatible family, were closer than ever after the burning of the shrine, and Sensei prayed that they would always remain strong in their faith.

Some weeks later she suffered an attack of arthritis, and Saburo came to see her. He was on the point of tears.

"Oh, Sensei!" he said, kneeling by her bed. "Forgive me! I am the cause of your sickness. It's my disobedience which has brought affliction to you."

"What makes you think that?" Sensei asked. "What's the trouble?"

The schoolboy found it difficult to express himself, but finally he told her that he was miserable because, while everyone else in the family was winning souls to Christ, he had done nothing. "I don't know what mistakes I've made," he said. "But I'm sure that's why you're sick."

Sensei comforted him, telling that his failure to win souls had not caused her illness. "Why does it seem hard for you to get souls?" she asked.

He looked at her unhappily. "I'm the youngest boy in our school," he said, "and it's difficult to talk to the other boys about Christian matters. They don't want to listen to me."

Sensei gave him some suggestions about showing friendship to the others, and they prayed over the problem. In a practical manner, she suggested that he pray for a single schoolmate, and then seek to follow that boy in whatever way the Lord would direct. Saburo rode off on his bicycle feeling better.

A few days later he attended a class in soul-winning which Sensei was teaching. The text was Christ's injunction: "Ye shall be fishers of men."

To Sensei's secret amusement, Saburo prayed: "Lord, give me a big fish instead of all the little ones I've missed!"

He confided to Sensei that the "big fish" he was after was a lad named Yamakuchi, the prefect of his class and a fine athlete. "I've been carrying his books," Saburo said. "And putting them in his locker."

That was not such a small matter. The weather was extremely hot, and the school was on the top of a high, steep hill. The school books were heavy.

"Yamakuchi isn't biting, though," the boy said gloomily. "He finally asked me why I was toting his books for him, and I told him he was the 'big fish' I wanted to catch. When he wanted to know what I meant, I told him I wanted him to come here for meetings, and that I thought maybe if I carried his books for a couple of weeks, he would. He said nothing doing!"

"You keep your faith up!" Sensei told him. "I think you may catch your 'big fish' for the Lord."

The next Sunday, Saburo, his face wreathed in smiles, came

leading a tall, good-looking boy to Sunday school.

"This is my friend, Yamakuchi," he said to Sensei, and then as soon as he could get her aside, he whispered to her: "He says he's only coming this one time in return for my carrying his books, so give him everything you've got this morning!"

Sensei chuckled and promised to try. She made the gospel story as clear as she could, and Yamakuchi was interested in spite of himself. He returned the following three Sundays, and after the third, professed his faith. Saburo was jubilant. He had finally become a real soul-winner.

Not long after that, Mr. Miki resigned from the Stock Exchange. When he mounted the rostrum that morning, members expected the usual announcement that trading could begin. Instead they heard their president say: "I am not here to tell you that the Exchange is open," he said. "I am here to tell you that this is the last time I will appear before you in any official capacity. I have a new Master, the Lord Jesus Christ, and I feel that I cannot continue in this work since I have come to know Him. I am therefore resigning as of this day."

The president's announcement caused plenty of comment. The story was told in business circles throughout Japan, and many people shook their heads and wondered "what had happened to Miki."

The decision cost the family a considerable amount in worldly goods. Their wardrobes dwindled. Other places of employment were found for the servants, and Mrs. Miki and her daughters took over the unaccustomed household chores. The sons did the work which gardeners had once done. Yet, though their life was much simpler, they were happier.

Having faced the first problem, Mr. Miki now turned to the task of breaking up his secret home in Osaka. Only Sensei was his confidante here, and she was not surprised one night when he asked her to go with him to Osaka.

The home to which he took her was lovely. A stately Japanese women in her middle thirties welcomed her graciously. She wore a lovely hand-embroidered light blue kimono, such as might have been worn by a woman of high rank. Sensei felt guilty for being impressed by her, but she could not help admit that her hostess was as charming as she was beautiful.

A maid took Sensei's coat, and she was ushered into a large living room. A costly Chinese rug covered the tatami floor. A glowing fire in the hibachi set off the beautiful teakettle, hanging from its three-pronged rack, singing invitingly. Sensei was given the place of honor—a handsome lacquered stool, decorated with inlaid mother of pearl. Tea was served immediately in fragile Japanese cups without handles.

To her surprise, Sensei noticed a leather-bound Japanese Bible and a copy of *Daily Light* on the desk near her. She assumed that they belonged to Mr. Miki.

The maid brought the ingredients for *sukiyaki,* and prepared it for them. As the dinner proceeded, Sensei was more and more deeply impressed by the gentility of her hostess.

When the dishes and utensils were cleared away after the meal, the geisha bowed to Mr. Miki. "I would like to talk to Smith Sensei," she said in her low, pleasant voice. Bowing, he withdrew to another room, and the geisha turned to Sensei. "I have seen this day coming for some time," she said, her beautiful face serene. "I knew that the time would come when Mr. Miki and I must separate, and since he has become a Christian, this time cannot be delayed."

She turned and picked up the Bible and a notebook which lay beneath it. "When you conducted your classes in the Miki home, Mr. Miki took notes in the study," she said. "The next night he always brought them to me, and we shared them."

Her graceful hand smoothed the cover of the notebook. "I have kept up with everything you have taught," she said. "I even know the hymns that were sung. And I have read the Bible for myself." She looked across at Sensei. "I wish to become a Christian myself tonight."

Sensei talked with her for a long time, and it was very evident that her hostess knew and understood the demands of God. Mr. Miki was recalled to the room, and the three of them prayed together. Then the former geisha girl accepted Christ.

She and Mr. Miki parted that night. Because of their love for Another, they never saw each other again. Sensei learned later that the new convert moved to quarters where geisha girls made their homes, and there became a missionary of a kind to her own.

8

Kazue's Deep Trouble

The day for Kazue's wedding was approaching. The young man was a professed Christian, though his parents were Buddhists. Although he had been chosen for her by her father, Kazue was excited and happy as plans for the wedding went forward.

There was a less personal excitement among the children at Sunrise Home at this time, an excitement which all of Japan shared. A Crown Prince had been born to Emperor Hirohito and his Empress.

Four daughters had previously been born to the royal couple, but since only male heirs were eligible to succeed to the throne, the hope for a son had been high throughout the land. Indeed, great pressure to take a concubine had been brought to bear on the Emperor at one time, but he had refused, saying that he loved his wife and that they were content with their girls until God should give them a son.

Then the 23rd day of December, Sensei was wakened early by the children who came pouring into her room.

"Get out quickly, Sensei!" they cried. "The Crown Prince has arrived! The *gogai* has been going through the streets crying the news, telling everybody about it!"

Sensei was as delighted as the children. "We must put up the flags!" she declared, jumping from bed and pulling on her dressing gown.

The children ran to get the bamboo poles, and Sensei helped them tie on special purple silk cords with purple tassels. Then they unfurled the gay Japanese flags with their white fields and red circles of the Rising Sun.

The children clustered around Sensei. "What are we going to send for a present?" they asked.

"I wasn't thinking of sending anything," Sensei said, looking ruefully at Mercy Coles.

"Oh, we *must* give him something!" the children cried. Gifts of some sort are given at every occasion in Japan, and this was certainly a special occasion.

Sensei and Mercy tried to explain that the royal baby would have many fine gifts, and that he would need nothing they might send to him. But the children were not satisfied. They rummaged through a box of hand-knitted and crocheted articles sent to the Home by friends, but Sensei explained firmly that nothing there was suitable.

The children were perplexed. "But aren't we going to do *anything?*" they asked. "We prayed a long time for a Crown Prince!"

Finally, more to please the children than anything else, Sensei sat down and wrote out a telegram in English. It read: "Sunrise Home children and staff rejoice with you in God's gift of a son."

A delegation of the children scampered off with Mercy to send the telegram. Forty-eight hours later Sensei received a telegram from the Imperial Palace. She was asked to appear at a government office in Kobe.

"Now what do you suppose I've done?" she asked Mercy. "Perhaps it wasn't proper to send that wire."

Mercy tried to reassure her, but both women were nervous when Sensei set off for Kobe the next day. To her amazement, she found a beautiful bouquet of flowers and a huge basket of fruit waiting for her, and she was told there were two big cases of food—one of powdered milk and the other of cookies—for the children, as well as a note of thanks from the Empress and a gift of money. Sensei was so overwhelmed she could scarcely express her thanks, and there was a real celebration at the Home that evening.

Gradually the excitment over the Crown Prince gave way to the closer-to-home excitement over Kazue's wedding. The children, who adored Kazue, wanted reports every time she came to the Home. Was the wedding gown of traditional black silk, intricately embroidered, finished? Were all the sets of kimonos made ready?

Smiling, Kazue assured them that everything was in order, but the smile left her face when she was alone with Sensei. "If my fiancé is really a Christian," she asked, "why is he now objecting to a Christian wedding?"

Sensei said that she did not know he was, and Kazue nodded unhappily. "He seems afraid of offending his parents," she said. "You know they're strong Buddhists. But I cannot be married unless it is a Christian wedding," she said. "Please pray with me, Sensei."

Sensei did, and the young girl left for home in better spirits, but the matter continued to trouble Sensei. She confided in Mercy Coles, and the two of them prayed together.

Their prayers seemed to have been answered, for objections to the Christian ceremony ceased. The day of the wedding arrived. Sensei and Mercy were among the honored guests. The home was beautiful with flowers which the children had cut. Kazue, her face radiant, was dressed in her elegant kimona with her *obi* tied in a butterfly bow. Her eyes glowed with faith as the vows were exchanged, but Sensei could not help but notice the rigid lines in which the faces of the groom's parents were set.

Kazue was, of course, looking forward to establishing her own home, but for financial reasons she and her bridegroom would have to live with his parents for a time.

As she entered their home, she bowed low as was the custom, and told her parents-in-law that she wanted to be a good daughter to them.

Her mother-in-law spoke harshly. "Here is our family shrine," she said. "Bow down and worship!"

Kazue was stunned. She turned, bewildered, to her groom, but his eyes did not meet hers, and he said nothing. It was all too evident that he was dominated by his mother. Kazue felt sick, but quietly and firmly she refused to make obeisance to the shrine.

Already angry because her son had married a Christian, the

mother-in-law was now raised to such a pitch of fury that she began systematic persecution of Kazue. Mornings, after Kazue had prepared the breakfast, the men left the house. As soon as they were gone, the mother-in-law began haranguing and mistreating Kazue. Day after day she forced her to sit in a cupboard where the bedclothing was stored.

"Stay there until you see things in a better light!" the mother-in-law ordered, slamming and locking the door, keeping her confined there until it was time for the men to come home.

Kazue did not tell her husband of this treatment, but she begged that they find a place of their own. He replied petulantly that he did not want to leave home, and that if Kazue would only put herself out a little, she could get on very well with his mother.

Silently Kazue bore her torture week after week. She complained to no one. The situation went on for months until one day Kazue suffered a severe hemorrhage of the lungs. No longer able to endure the treatment, Kazue sent word to her mother that she was ill.

Her mother was shocked when she saw her daughter. The mother-in-law shrugged indifferently, saying that Kazue had not found the food in their house good enough for her and had refused to eat. Kazue did not contradict the lie.

Mrs. Miki took her daughter at once to a doctor who diagnosed tuberculosis. The Mikis, sensing that there was more behind their daughter's illness than they had been told, insisted that she return to Akashi with them. Neither Kazue's husband nor her in-laws offered any argument. They seemed glad enough to be rid of her.

Kazue was taken by ambulance, and when they reached Akashi, she asked that they stop at Sunrise Home long enough for her to see Sensei. Sensei's heart was twisted with grief when she saw her young friend, but she asked no questions. She pressed Kazue's hand and told her that she and everyone else at Sunrise Home would be praying for her, and the sweetness in Kazue's face deepened.

Whenever Sensei could, she visited Kazue. The luminous beauty of the young girl's face seemed to grow deeper as the months passed. She spent hours of her time praying for friends and relatives, and she guarded a worn little notebook in which she kept the names of hundreds of people she carried in her heart and remembered in intercessory prayer.

In the notebook she recorded some of her thoughts in the form of devotional messages, and they were later published in a booklet which was called *Kazue's Diary* and was distributed throughout Japan. It was instrumental in leading many to a knowledge of Christ.

High on the list of those for whom Kazue prayed was her nurse, an obdurate pagan who told Kazue in no uncertain terms what she thought of Christianity. "It will do you no good to pray for me!" she warned.

But Kazue continued her prayers. Much as the nurse disagreed with her patient's religion, the dour woman was fond of Kazue, and one day to please her, she attended a Bible meeting where she heard a message on the Cross. The arrow of conviction pierced her hard exterior, and she crept off to bed that night almost in tears. Toward morning, unable to wait any longer, she went to her patient's bedside, and on her knees begged to be saved. Before the dawn turned to daylight, Kazue led her to Christ.

When the anniversary of Mr. Miki's conversion came, Kazue wanted the family to have a "birthday" party for him. She was not well enough to help with any of the preparations, but when the joyous day arrived, she joined the relatives and friends, Sensei among them, in the dining room.

The long table was laden with delicacies. There were meats of many kinds, mushrooms and eggs, ginger and dainty cakes and fruit. Mr. Miki spoke of the transformation Christ had made in the lives of all of his family, and there was great rejoicing. Kazue was too ill to stay for the whole party, and when she went back to her room, Sensei went with her.

They sat quietly, not talking much, but there was great communion between them, and the room seemed to be filled with the radiance of their faith.

When it was time for Sensei to leave, Kazue asked her to bend close, and she kissed Sensei's forehead, though such outward shows of affection are rare among the Japanese.

"You introduced me to the Savior," she whispered.

Tears stung Sensei's eyes. "And your life has made other lives bright," she said, her voice rich with feeling. "God has used you greatly."

9

She "Being Dead yet Speaketh"

Spring came to Sunrise Home and the lovely Inland Sea area. Sensei, knowing that cherry blossoms would soon bring a new dimension of glory, decided that this was the time of year to gather all the missionaries in that part of Japan together for a spiritual retreat. She wished suddenly that Al could come, too—she would like very much to show him the Japan she loved, and at this, its most beautiful time of year. But it could not be, and Sensei put the wish from her.

The missionaries to Japan came from far and near. Jim and Clara Cuthbertson were there. Other missionaries, some Japanese and some English and Irish, were present. Her old friend

Adelaide Soal came, and Sensei could not help but notice the lines of weariness in her face.

"The Lord's work is not easy," Adelaide said, evading a more direct answer to her friend's questions.

Sensei had not devised a formal program for the gathering. There was no chairman, and there was no order of service. Instead sessions began with hymn singing, one after another suggesting a song for Mercy to play. Singing was followed by a time of prayer when those present sought the Lord to draw them closer in fellowship with Him and with one another.

At one meeting Jim Cuthbertson spoke from the Scripture passage describing the Lord's post-Resurrection appearance, stressing the phrase: "He showed them His hands and His feet," and emphasizing the central teaching of Calvary.

"We are His disciples," he said, "and we are used as His hands and feet to spread His gospel and carry out acts of kindness to the needy."

The days of the meetings were joyous ones. Everyone pitched in with kitchen and household chores. There were walks through the beautiful countryside and silent periods of meditation. Personal differences which may have existed were cleared away. The five days were a time of renewal for all of them.

"It has been a veritable Pentecost," Irene said to Adelaide. "The Holy Ghost has come down to us these days in mighty power!"

Adelaide did not answer then, but when she returned to her mission in Maizuru, she wrote Sensei a letter. "When the conference began," she said, "I almost dreaded returning to this area, for the work had grown almost unbearably difficult. But now everything has changed. I spoke to the people about the experience at Akashi, and a similar time of revival blessing broke out here. It was as though the renewal of faith which we found reached out to others."

Sensei nodded to herself. That was what had happened. She made a mental note to hold springtime meetings each year at Akashi.

In the autumn of that year, 1932, Sensei returned again to England on furlough. She said good-by to Kazue, feeling that she would never see her again.

As usual, furlough time brought little rest to Sensei, for she was always in demand for lectures and talks. When one of the Board members told her that she really should take a little more time for herself, she laughed. "Oh, this is my strength!" she said. "It's better than a rest cure!"

While in Britain she decided that she would visit Amy Carmichael's work in South India on her way back to Japan. Ever since she had read Miss Carmichael's books, she had wanted to meet her.

Consequently, when her year away from Japan was nearly up, she sailed from Liverpool aboard the *Terukuni Maru*. She thought about Miss Carmichael considerably on the voyage. Unconsciously, the patrician Irishwoman had had a good deal of influence on Irene, who had always been interested in her work to save children who had been sold by their families into temples.

"I could have visited her at Donahvur when I first went out to Japan," she thought. "But something kept me from it. I think if I'd gone, I would have modeled my work after hers, and it has been better for Sunrise Home to develop along its own lines without any copying."

Sensei had written to Miss Carmichael that after she docked, she wanted to travel by oxcart rather than train from Tinnevelly to Donahvur so that she might actually experience some of the hardships early Indian missionaries had known. It was a quaint request, and in view of Sensei's eye problem, probably not a sensible one. But when something was spiritually important to Sensei, practicality came second. The request was granted, and the cart was waiting on her arrival.

It was made of rough boards and drawn by two oxen. There was no seat, so Sensei, not as young as she once was, sat on the floor. She soon found that the going was decidedly rough. The roads were muddy and rutted. When it was necessary to ford a river, the oxen descended ponderously down the banks and waded into the river, splashing it in waves over their hapless passenger. At one fording, the beasts stopped in midstream for a bath and bucolic frolic. The cart was thrown about, and plump Sensei, who expected to be tossed into the muddy water at any moment, was rolled about cruelly.

"It's a good thing I'm well-padded!" she gasped. "Oh, my! Poor Adelaide would really be the worse for wear!"

By the time she reached Tinnevelly, she was bruised and aching. "Well," she said ruefully, "I asked for it! And I can't say it wasn't a good experience. Now I know what the missionaries to India suffered in their early days!"

Miss Carmichael, who was confined to her bed these days, welcomed her visitor, and the staff went out of their way to make the visit a memorable one. She was shown the sights and treated like royalty.

"Bless me!" she exclaimed. "I'll be too spoiled to go back to work!" And she added with a twinkle: "Now isn't it lovely of the Lord to let us be spoiled a little?"

Evenings at Donahvur there were prayer meetings, and at one of them Sensei rose and prayed for Miss Carmichael who, as she said, had been "set aside." She thought she heard a suppressed titter, but she couldn't for the life of her imagine why. When she went to her room that night, she opened one of Amy Carmichael's books, and she discovered the reason for the held-back laughter! Miss Carmichael believed firmly that there was no such thing as being "set aside" in God's work! The book went on to say:

> "God never wastes His servants' time.
> God never wastes His servants' toil.
> God never wastes His servants' pain.
> God never wastes His servants' gifts."

He may transfer you from one sphere of action to another," the book declared, "but He never wastes anything put at His disposal."

"Oh, dear me!" Sensei thought. "I hope no one will report what I said to Miss Carmichael!" Then she studied the words again, nodding at their message. "She's right!" she said out loud with conviction. "I will never use that phrase, 'set aside,' again!"

She spent many long hours talking to Miss Carmichael, and she found the visit highly inspirational. Before she left, she gave a check for ten pounds to the Donahvur Fellowship.

As she embarked for Japan, one of the staff members handed her an envelope. When she was settled in her cabin, she opened it. It contained a sacrificial offering from one of the Donahvur missionaries for Sunrise Home. The check was for ten pounds!

"Lord, what's the use of my trying to give You anything!" Sensei exclaimed. "I gave that ten pounds, and here it is back again!"

It was a few days before Christmas when Sensei reached Kobe again. The Sunrise staff and the older children were all gathered on the wharf waiting to greet her, and they had a happy reunion.

"How is Kazue?" Sensei asked Mercy Coles anxiously as soon as she could.

Mercy's face saddened. "Very ill, Sensei. She's completely bed-ridden now. She's waiting to see you. She vowed she would wait until you came home."

At the first possible moment, Sensei hastened to see her friend. Kazue's eyes lighted with joy as the two clasped hands. "I knew I would see you before I go Home," she said. "I asked God to let me."

Sensei spent every moment she could spare with the dying girl. She learned that Kazue's husband, who really loved her, was defying his mother; coming often to see his young wife, and Sensei was thankful.

One wild March day of wind and rain, Kazue suffered hemorrhage. Sensei rushed to her bedside. Kazue's face looked waxen, and she was in great pain, but she was smiling bravely and her spirit seemed to glow with a new intensity of faith.

She asked that she be left alone with Sensei, and then, her voice barely audible, she asked Sensei to take her diary and without looking at it destroy certain pages, which she listed. Sensei did as she was asked, and the dying girl seemed relieved.

"Hold my hand, Sensei," she whispered.

Sensei called the family members back softly and took her place beside Kazue, holding her hand gently but firmly.

"When you feel my hold relax," Kazue whispered, "you will know that I have put my hand into the hand of Jesus. He will come to meet me."

Exhausted by the effort to speak, she struggled for breath, and then went on: "He went through death for me . . . But I will only pass through the shadow. . . ." Her eyes turned to her father and mother, then to her husband. "It will be the Resurrection," she whispered.

Her hand went limp. Sensei bowed her head. Sweet, faithful Kazue was with her Savior.

Kazue's body was prepared for the coffin in Japanese fashion, and it was placed in the front room on the bier. The day of her burial, the little band of mourners stood with bowed heads about their loved one, prayer in their hearts. There was a commotion at the door, and Kazue's mother-in-law burst in. She looked wild and disheveled, and she threw herself down by the coffin, weeping and crying.

"Kazue, forgive me!" she wailed. "Open your eyes! Speak to me! Give me forgiveness!"

There was confusion in the room. No one knew why the mother-in-law was so distraught. Her son pulled her to her feet, trying to quiet her.

"What is it?" he asked. "Why are you asking forgiveness in this way?"

"I killed her!" the wretched woman cried. "Don't you know that she lies in her coffin because of my cruelty?"

Blankness and shock showed on the faces of the others, and the woman cried out: "Did she never tell you? Did she never speak of what I did to her?" Then the whole story poured out.

The Diary pages! Sensei thought. *She had confided in it. That's why she wanted the pages destroyed!*

"Kazue never told us," Mrs. Miki choked. "She never spoke one word."

Kazue's husband made a strangled sound, and Sensei, her heart shaken, turned to the woman. "Kazue forgave you long ago," she said. "Now God wants to forgive you. Turn to Him now! Find forgiveness and life!"

The others got to their knees, and Sensei prayed. The woman knelt, too, and Sensei spoke with her quietly of Christ's willingness to forgive her and give her life and peace.

"How can He ever forgive *me?*" she cried.

They prayed together, and the mother-in-law confessed her new found faith in Christ. Even in death, Kazue's witness was heard.

"She being dead yet speaketh," Sensei whispered.

10

New Home at Akashi

Sensei was deeply touched by Kazue's death, but life in the Home had to go on, and with thirty little girls to tend and care for, that life had to be ordered. Sensei had learned a great deal about managing since that first little baby girl had arrived at the first Sunrise Home so many years ago. There were jobs for everyone in the Home, from the older girls who attended high school to the preschool "Tinies," as Sensei called them in British fashion. By American, or even Japanese, standards, Sensei was a disciplinarian, but she was not a martinet. Her sense of order was always tempered with oceans of love and affection that sprang spontaneously from her warm Irish heart.

Sensei had made some changes over the years. The girls now wore uniforms, usually made by loving hands back in England or Ireland. For the older girls, the uniforms were usually pale yellow or blue jersey; for the younger ones, red or pink. The teenagers would never have worn the latter colors, for they were reserved by Japanese custom for the very young or the very old. When a Japanese man or woman reached his sixty-first birthday, there was always a gift of red garments—a shirt for a man or a kimono for a woman. In the years when the wives of American servicemen of the Occupation forces appeared in red coats or dresses, the Japanese regarded this as a juvenile expression. As for Sensei's children, there was one color that all of them could wear, and that was Sensei's favorite—green! Sensei saw that every one of them had one uniform of this color, and when all thirty of them appeared in green on the streets of Akashi, the local residents would say: "Here come the Jesus girls!"

The girls themsleves decided what color they would wear to school on a given day. If the older girls chose yellow, they all appeared in that color. The younger ones might choose red. But all of a given age wore the same color on a particular day.

This was all part of Sensei's eagerness to teach them neatness and to make them stand out as Christian witnesses. She wanted them to be known and to demonstrate by their good behavior that Christianity affected all areas of life and conduct.

Sensei taught each child a sense of responsibility. She expected them to perform their household chores dutifully and without grumbling, and as a result, they did. She stressed constantly the importance of doing well in school, although Japanese children generally strive for such accomplishment. Her goal included a high school education for every child.

The youngsters attended grammar school with the other children of the community, but high school was a problem.

"We have to establish our own!" Sensei told Mercy Coles

with conviction. "That's the only solution!"

"But how can we?" Mercy said. "Who will teach the classes?"

"I'll find a way!" Sensei said.

And she did. With the help of the principal of a near-by government high school for girls, Sensei obtained permission from the National Department of Education to conduct high school classes at Sunrise Home. Then she enlisted the help of five teachers from Akashi. Mercy Coles and Sensei herself supplemented the teaching staff.

It was a great day when the first Sunrise teen-agers started their high school education; a greater day when the first group graduated. This was a cause for celebration, and Sensei arranged a ceremony to mark the event. A service was held in the big meeting room of the Home. A platform was built at one end of the room, and on one side of it, Oka-san arranged a beautiful bouquet in a large jar. The central part of the bouquet was a spreading branch of pine. In front of it were blue iris, pink sweet peas and white and yellow narcissus. On the piano there was a vase of pink carnations, and elsewhere in the room great bouquets of tulips and tiger lilies added to the festive air.

"Now isn't it lovely!" Sensei said to Mercy when the decorations were completed. "Won't this give our little Sunbeams the grandest send-off! I'm that proud of them, Mercy!"

"And you should be," Mercy smiled. "You've raised them all, with the Lord's help."

On the day of graduation the girls came forward to receive their diplomas from the headmaster. Each gave him a formal bow an then turned to Jim Cuthbertson who had come to officiate. Taking the diplomas, in both hands and holding them level with their faces, the girls continued to bow, in true Japanese fashion, walking backwards to their seats. There were speeches and songs, and then refreshments of tea, sandwiches and cakes. The youngsters were radiant, and Sensei was as happy as any of them.

"It's a dream come true!" she told Mercy that night when they retired. "And isn't it grand how many have enrolled in the JEB Bible School? Oh, they'll serve the Lord as fine witnesses, that I know!"

With the graduation of the first high school class over, life settled down to its usual routine at Sunrise Home, but now a new project came into being. During a stay at the Karuizawa rest home, Sensei encountered Merrill Vories, an American architect turned missionary. He stressed vocational training, and at the time Sensei met him, he was demonstrating an electric washing machine.

Sensei was entranced. It was just what was needed at the Home! Hopefully she asked the price. It was $400. Sensei's heart sank. "I can never make that!" she exclaimed, and gave the shiny machine a long, wistful look.

"I'll tell you what I'll do," Vories told Sensei. "I'm showing this machine this summer—it's a demonstrator. At the end of the season I'll let you have it for half price."

The sum of $200 was nearly as far out of reach as $400 for Sensei, but still, what a bargain! She reported her find to the girls on her return to Sunrise Home, and they were enthusiastic.

"Let's pray the Lord will help us find the needed money to buy the machine," Sensei said.

The older girls looked at each other. They had not been brought up by Sensei for nothing. As part of their training program, some of the older girls planned the meals, did the shopping, and helped with the cooking. They had a budget for each week, and it could not have been called large, but now the girls made their plan. They would set aside a little each week from the money allotted for meals, and this would start the washing machine fund.

"Let's keep it a secret from Sensei!" Noriko said excitedly. "Maybe we can save enough to really *buy* the washer and give it to Sensei as a present!"

The girls were excited, and they set to work on their plan. Never did anyone work harder to cut a budget! They couldn't skimp on the food, but in those next months they devised many new menus which cost next to nothing. Every week the money they saved was set aside, and the fund grew. At last they had saved enough to buy the sample washer! What a pile of money it was!

Eyes bright, they carried the fund to Sensei.

"What's this?" she cried. "Wherever did you get such a vast sum as all this!"

The girls' excitement spilled out of them. All talking at once, they told Sensei what they had done. "It's for the washer!" they cried. "We saved every yen all by ourselves, Sensei!"

Sensei's eyes misted. "Bless you!" she said. "It's a grand thing you've done! I'm proud of you all—it's that smart and good you are!"

The washing machine was bought that week, and it occupied a place of honor at Sunrise Home. Every time Sensei used it she thought of the youngsters who, by their own initiative, and economies had earned the money to buy it. It was a shining star in the crown of events that marked the life at Sunrise Home.

But it wasn't only the older children who put stars in this crown. The younger ones put them there, too. As Christmas approached in that year of the washing machine, the little girls sitting on their gay-colored cushions in a circle about the hibachi talked about what they would get as gifts.

"Perhaps there will be no dolls from England or America this year," Keiko worried, her small face intent.

"Yes, there *will* be!" Akiko said. "I saw them in Sensei's cupboard one day when I was in her room. She slid the door back a little too far and I really and truly saw them!"

A chorus of happy satisfaction greeted this news, and the youngsters chattered about the coveted presents.

"I really need a new doll," Kaori said. "Mine is getting *so* old!"

"My doll's eyes have come out!" another child said.

"I want a doll with blond curly hair," Hanako cried, clasping her small hands together in delightful expectation.

"And I want some new doll clothes!" Micheko exclaimed.

At that point Sensei joined them. The youngsters gulped back their chatter, for it would never do to let Sensei know that they had discovered the hoped-for dolls.

Sensei, very well aware of what the excited talk had been about, sat down on the *zabuton* with them.

"I have something to tell you," she began, looking into their small happy faces. "Not far away there is a village where some poor little children live. Some of our missionaries are going down there for the first time to tell them about Jesus and His love."

The children looked solemn, and Sensei went on: "These poor children will have no Christmas presents and no treats. There won't be any stockings for them on Christmas morning, because they are not Christians." She looked at the children. "I wonder if you would like to help these children by giving them some of your old toys and dolls? Of course," she said, "you will be getting some new ones. Will you think about what I've said and talk it over?"

With a smile and a nod, Sensei left them.

The youngsters looked at each other. They agreed that of course they would like to give their old dolls to the village children.

But suddenly Hanako spoke out. "I will *not* give my old doll!" she said, looking at them.

The children were astonished. "Hana, how can you be so selfish!" Akiko cried, and the others joined in.

Hanako faced them, her look determined. "Giving to those children is like giving to Jesus," she said. "And I don't want to give Him my *old* doll! I want to give Him my new one!"

The youngsters stared at her, and then understanding came to their eyes. "Oh, Hanako!" Akika cried. "I'll do that, too! I don't need a new doll!"

One by one, the other youngsters agreed. They rushed to tell Sensei.

"You know that means you won't have any dolls for Christmas," she said, very proud of them all. "Will you be happy with your old ones?"

"We *will* be!" the children chorused. "Sensei, we *will* be!"

"I know what well do!" Hanako cried. "We'll give all our old dolls to you, and on Christmas day you can give them to us. We'll *pretend* they're all new!"

The children clapped and chattered with excitement at the idea. They rushed off for their dolls and took them back to Sensei.

"Bless you!" Sensei said, gathering the dolls into her arms. "You've made the Lord Jesus very happy!"

Satisfied, the children scampered away, and Sensei carried the dolls up to her room. After prayers that evening, she told the older children what had happened, and they promptly set out on a project of their own. In the days left before Christmas, they spent every spare minute fixing up the old dolls and making new wardrobes for them.

The new dolls were taken to the village for the poor children, and on Christmas morning, two sets of little girls were filled with happiness. And in the village where the new dolls had gone, many parents were touched by the expression of love from the little Sunbeams. Not a few of them came forward on the Christ Child's birthday to accept Him in their hearts, and Sensei's heart overflowed with happiness and with love.

The years at Sunrise Home passed swiftly. Sensei woke one morning realizing that the Home had been operating for ten years.

She turned to Mercy. "We're getting old!" she chuckled. "I think we must have a celebration to mark all these good years!"

Mercy laughed. "I've yet to see a time you didn't see a reason for celebration!" she said. "But I agree with you, Sensei. This is a good time!"

All the officials of Akashi were invited. The many friends they had made among the townspeople were included, and missionaries in the area were sent invitations, too. Everyone who could possibly make it was present on the gala day.

There were speeches and testimonials. There was singing by the Sunrise children, accompanied by one of Mercy's prize pupils. Kioka San, the agent who so long ago had aided Sensei in the purchase of the property, testified that he and his wife and two daughters had all become Christians. Mr. Miki spoke. "We are all Smith Sensei's children," he concluded. One of the

Irene Webster-Smith as a young woman in Ireland before she received her call to serve God in Japan.

The lovely gardens of the home of Count and Countess Makeno, controller of the Imperial Household, at Maizuru, served as the playground of the children of the Sunrise Home for several years. Here (seated at left) Irene Webster-Smith and her good friend, Adelaide Soal (seated at right) are shown with some of their charges and Japanese helpers.

Through the generosity of Dr. Hezekiah Saiki, a distinguished gynecologist and obstetrician, two little Japanese houses at Kyoto were placed at the disposal of Sensei when she and Miss Soal launched Sunrise Home "on faith" in February, 1922. Miss Soal (at right of pram) and Sensei (extreme right) were soon caring for seven babies all under a year old.

An abandoned hospital that the neighbors said was haunted was transformed into the expanded Sunrise Home at Akashi looking south toward the romantically beautiful Inland Sea. Sensei purchased the property from an elderly Buddhist priest in a town where Christians were not wanted. But soon the Home was echoing with the shouts of happy children and the community gracefully accepted the "Jesus people." Miss Mercy Coles (left of rock at center) and Sensei (seated at right of center) are shown here with some of the Sunrise children and their high school teachers.

Little Sachiko (with bow in her hair), shown with her friend Kyoko, prayed for a walking and talking doll, quite unknown to Sensei who was spending a furlough in Great Britain. When Sensei brought the doll back to Japan, Kyoko insisted that it belonged to Sachiko. Later Sachiko (right) grew up and married a Japanese evangelist. The five little girls (below) prayed for a trip to the seashore after they suffered an attack of whooping cough. They are shown with their schoolbags strapped to their backs.

Kazue Miki, daughter of a wealthy Buddhist family at Akashi, attended a Bible class at the Sunrise Home and became a Christian. Later all the members of her family followed suit and forsook their family gods.

When most missionaries might think of retirement, Irene Webster-Smith plunged into a ministry among the teeming throngs of university students in downtown Tokyo. For the Japanese equivalent of $18,000, she bought a piece of property on which she erected the Ochanomizu Student Christian Center, now valued at more than $1,000,000. (Below) Sensei explains a Bible passage to a group of students.

The characteristic exuber
of Sensei is shown as she la
with Pioneer Girls camper
Port Sydney, Ontario, during
wartime stay in the Un
States and Canada. Below
is with the author at his h
in Merion Station, Pennsylva
in the summer of 1964.

As she approaches 80, Sensei continues to speak at public gatherings, counsels with university students, entertains her Sunrise "girls" who now have grown children of their own. A life of rich and varied ministry has compensated for some of the suffering and loss that she has known.

carpenters who had been converted while he worked on the building repairs spoke. It was a glorious and happy occasion.

At the end of the day, a young man from Akashi said the words which were in everyone's heart: "No one could have been here today and still doubt that we worship the living God!"

"Amen," Sensei said, and her heart was happy.

It was not long after this meeting when the typhoon season began. It came every year, this season of heavy rains and tempestuous winds, and Sunrise Home had known the vengeance of the storms before.

But this year the storm struck with greater violence. As the winds rose and the rain began to lash down, Sensei and the staff hurried to make what preparations they could. But the fury of the storm rose. The sea that lay across the narrow road from them boiled like a cauldron. Screaming wind, driving the rain ahead of it, lashed at the Home. Water streamed through the windows and doors which gave way before it.

Sensei herded her children into the downstairs dining room which was the safest and driest place in the Home.

She took the older girls aside. "Sing!" she commanded them. "That's the only way we'll keep the little ones from being afraid."

Their young voices started the hymns. Sensei and the other staff members rushed to battle the storm. Rugs were pulled up. Draperies came down. Bedding and towels were thrown onto floors to sop up the flood. A big window was wrenched from its socket and hung flapping. Desperately, Sensei tried to hold it in place, but it tore loose, sending a shower of splintering glass over her.

"Are you hurt?" Mercy cried.

Sensei shook her head. "Keep working!" she ordered.

Through the broken windows she saw tile, slates, gutters and drain pipes go flying through the air, twisting and turning as the wind drove them. She heard the stucco falling from the back of the house, and looking up saw the huge iron lid of the water tank sail through space. A prayer burst from her lips as it careened past the window.

Through the storm, neighbors, leaving their own houses, battled their way to Sunrise Home to try to help. A painter clawed his way onto the roof, trying to stop up the holes. Another man nailed the front door shut.

Three huge trees in front of the house crashed down. The wooden fence was ripped up by the wind and sent flying. The small house in the back where the old couple who, so long ago, had found a haven, was smashed to the ground, and Sensei thanked God that the faithful man and woman who had served Sunrise Home ever since that night were in the big house with the children.

Evening approached, and Sensei and the staff struggled to hold back the water which seemed bent on engulfing the Home. Huge chunks of the ceiling began to fall. Walls cracked and bulged.

"Lord, keep my family safe." Sensei prayed.

And at last the storm abated. The wind, screaming its last fury, died down. The lashing rain slacked off. Barefooted, soaked to the skin, weary to the point of exhaustion, Sensei gathered her children around her and thanked God they were safe. In all the devastation that the storm had done, only one child had been hurt, and she only slightly.

Somehow beds were made up for the children, and they were tucked three and four under a quilt. Sensei was too weary to sleep. Telling Mercy and Oka-san and the old couple to bed down with the children, she went out to the veranda. It was calm now, and she sat there in the moonlight, looking at the quiet sea. All that had happened seemed like a bad dream.

The next morning a steady procession of townspeople came to the Home, each wanting to know what he could do to help. But the havoc was too great. There was nothing that could really be done. The ceilings were down in eighteen of the twenty-three rooms. Walls were buckled. The roof was nearly gone.

One of the JEB missionaries in the area offered a temporary home for the youngest children, and they were sent off to him, an older girl going along to help care for them. The back of the Home was reasonably well preserved. This provided a shelter for the rest of Sensei's "family."

But Sensei knew she must find a new location. She turned to her Bible for guidance, and she read from II Chronicles 25:9: "The Lord is able to give thee much more than this." Sensei knew it was a promise from the Lord.

As she searched for a location for a new building, Sensei turned to her Bible again, and she found another verse which she felt was specific direction from Heaven: "The Lord gave me Haggai 1:8," she told Mercy. "It reads: 'Go up to the mountains and bring wood, and build the house; and I will take pleasure in it and I will be glorified, saith the Lord.' "

She looked tiredly at Mercy. "Where is the place, Mercy?" she asked.

"You will find it," Mercy answered.

And she did. It was about a mile above and beyond the original Sunrise Home. It was located in a lovely spot near a grove of pine trees, and it looked out on the Inland Sea. It was a more secluded area than the old home, and it was roomier. Also it was much less exposed to the usual track of the typhoons. Sensei obtained an option on the land, then wrote to friends back home for counsel on the wisdom of rebuilding.

One to whom she wrote was her sister Nell. At times before, Sensei had talked to her about selling the family home and using the proceeds for missionary work, but Nell and the other relatives had always been adamant against this. Nell cabled Sensei: "Go ahead and build."

The cable did not tell her specifically that those who remained of her family would now sell the home, yet she knew that was what it meant. And others—including Al—wrote, too, offering encouragement. Gifts began to pour in to carry out the work.

Sensei ordered workmen to tear down what was left of the old Sunrise Home, telling them to save whatever material might be used for the new building. They set to work; aghast they reported that there had been no iron bolts holding the joints together. It was a miracle that the building had not collapsed before.

Sensei wrote home to the JEB Board. "Friends at home," she said, "will not have the slightest conception of the endless consultations and the tramping around looking for land, before we were led to the spot the Lord showed was His choice for us. . . . Our new location is much farther away from the tram and train lines, sheltered from the sea by beautiful old pines, but with the same lovely view, only more distant, than we had in the old Home. We had some difficulty in getting the farmers to give up their rights to the property. Actually we had to buy more than I at first intended, but we really got it at a very reasonable price."

Work on the new Home started, and at about the same time a letter arrived from Amy Carmichael of Donahvur. "Make the new Home big enough," she wrote. "Or so build it that it can be made bigger. . . . I have made the mistake of trying to save money by some economy which later led to a larger expense. I am sure the Lord will guide you."

"And He is," Sensei wrote to her old friend Adelaide. "I do feel that He is."

As usual, once Sensei felt that the Lord was leading her, she moved with relentless speed. Merrill Vories, the missionary-architect who had sold her the washing machine, was given the job of drawing up the plans. A Christian Japanese builder was hired to do the construction work.

On January 22, 1938, Jim Cuthbertson, the architect, the builder, the pastor of a small church in Akashi and Sensei gathered at the new site for a prayer of dedication.

"Thank you, Lord," Sensei prayed, "for the provision of gifts from friends. By the eye of faith, I envision our new Home."

Work on the Home started, and two annoying situations promptly developed. First, the farmers of the community, who depended on night soil as fertilizer for their fields, learned that a modern sewage disposal system was being installed. They would be cheated of a great source of fertilizer, and they were angry.

"To think that all this will be lost to us!" they cried in indignation to Sensei as they besought her to change her plans. But Sensei stood firm. She knew the importance of sanitation, and much as she disliked getting off to a bad start with her new neighbors, this was an issue on which she would not compromise.

The second problem was the well. It was imperative that one be sunk and a good supply of water be assured for the new Home. Sensei called on a well diviner, and he said water could be found in three places on the property. After considerable discussion, Sensei decided on the place nearest the kitchen. A well digger and his crew of men and women arrived. The digging started.

Two men set to work first. When the well grew deeper, a pulley was set up over the wellsite. Buckets of earth were lifted by a rope attached to the pulley. The women manned the rope to hoist the buckets of dirt from the well. It was backbreaking, slow work.

When the men had dug down thirty feet, the well digger told Sensei that they had not found water.

"Keep on digging," she said.

The operation continued. Several times the well digger reported that they had not struck water. Each time Sensei replied: "Keep digging!"

By the time the well hole had been excavated to a depth of more than 100 feet, a deeper level than any of the surrounding wells, the foreman came to Sensei in desperation.

"It's no use!" he declared. "We must give up. Let us drill at one of the other locations."

Sensei was adamant. "I don't think I can," she said. "Because when we started sinking this well, I asked my God—the living God—to direct me, and I asked that not one yen of His money be wasted! A lot of people have given sacrificially to the building of this house and the digging of this well. We must go on."

The well digger looked at her wearily. "That is nonsense!" he said. "We must try another place."

She shook her head. "Be patient," she said. "And dig deeper."

With a shrug, he went back to his work. Every day at lunch time, Sensei visited the well. The women would be sitting there then, having their own frugal lunch, and Sensei told them about the living God she worshipped.

"He is a God of love," she said. "And a God of supply." She told them the story of Elijah's contest on Mount Carmel with the priests of Baal.

"My faith is like Elijah's," she said. "God will bring water to the well."

The crew went back to work. Sensei watched the women pulling on the rope to the tune of a rhythmic song they sang. But nothing came from the bottom of the well except slime.

Sensei mounted her bicycle and rode off to a clump of woods. There she "wrestled with the Lord" over the claim she had made to her pagan audience.

"Lord, if I have been wrong in being so persistent, forgive me," she prayed. "But don't let me down before these heathen!"

That evening the well digger clumped up to her to make his report.

"Now it is over!" he said with finality. "We are down 132 feet. We must stop digging. We have hit solid rock."

"That's wonderful!" Sensei beamed to the consternation of the foreman. "I was just reading this morning about how Moses struck the rock and out gushed the water! Please get someone to drill through that rock!"

He looked at her in disgust. "There's no use!" he snorted. But he had learned by this time he might as well do what Sensei wanted.

The next morning a new crew arrived to bore into the rock. None of them was enthusiastic, but a man went down into the well in a basket lowered by the rope. The boring began. The regular crew stood around waiting, all of them thinking that they were working for a crazy woman.

Sensei stayed away as long as she could, but her curiosity was too much for her. After about an hour she rushed down to the wellsite, and she was just in time to hear a muffled shout from the man in the well. He was shouting for the women to pull him up.

They moved with alacrity, and in moments he emerged, shouting and spluttering. He was drenched to the skin. Sensei's well had come in!

It proved to be one of the best in the area, and it never failed to produce a constant supply of pure fresh water. The farmers who had been irked about the sewage were invited to take whatever water they needed from the well, and it was not long before they had forgotten their grievances. Instead they tried to outdo each other in showing kindnesses to Sensei and the children when they came to the new Home. Sensei and her "Sunbeams" were never without all the fresh vegetables they could eat.

The exposure Sensei had suffered during the typhoon and the long seige of hard work while the new Home was being built finally told on Sensei. She suffered a painful attack of lumbago, followed by rheumatic fever. For almost two months she lay on her back, directing the work from her bed.

Finally by late spring, the handsome new two-story Home was completed. It was about the same dimensions as the old hospital structure, but solidly built. At one end of the building there was an L-shaped section which provided extra space for entertaining on the first floor and comfortable quarters for Sensei on the second. Friends and missionaries pitched in on moving day and, without too much disorder, all of the children and staff were transferred to their new quarters.

On June 6, 1938, a great gathering of friends attended the dedication of the new Home. It was an occasion for rejoicing and prayers of thanksgiving. Sensei recounted the history of her unique ministry to little girls, starting with the first two little houses in Kyoto and going on through the abandonment of the old hospital in Akashi to their new location. Through all these years, the growing needs of the Home had been met, and there had been a countless procession of episodes in which God had intervened "step by step."

At last, the work completed and the new Home operating smoothly, Sensei prepared to leave on furlough for Britain with a light heart and a warm sense of gratitude to God for His hand upon her during the eighteen years of her service in Japan. She little knew that the devastating conflict which was to engulf the world would bring vast changes to her own life.

11

Forced from Japan

In the year that Sensei was home on furlough, Hitler marched into Poland, and Great Britain declared war on Germany. Sensei's heart was heavy. The thought of bombed cities, of men and women dying, of children hungry and homeless weighed on her very soul, and she prayed that all men might one day know God as she did in her Quaker heart, so that all wars might be ended.

She felt that she must return to Japan, and somehow with the war's devastation so close, the urgency to return was even deeper, for her children were there. They had need of her.

Getting passage was next to impossible, and several times Sensei nearly gave up. But the urgency inside her kept driving her forward as though God Himself spoke to her and told her that she must hurry.

Finally, after months of tireless effort, she managed to book passage. She was not told the date of her sailing, or the place of embarkation, for all shipping movements were secret.

One day in late February she received word from a government office: "Proceed at once to Liverpool Station where you will be met."

Sensei had long been packed and ready, and she followed her orders. At eight o'clock that night she was waiting as she had been directed. An officer met her. They drove through the blacked-out streets to the pier, and in an eerie silence she was escorted aboard an unnamed vessel.

She was taken immediately to her cabin which she found she would be sharing with five other passengers. Their faces looked tense and drawn, and their greetings were subdued. The dark clouds of war lay over them, and it was not only the crowded conditions of the cabin, nor just the fact of sleeping so closely with strangers which kept them lying awake in their bunks that night. Every one knew how dangerous this journey was.

Some time in the middle of the night the ship came alive. The engines, throttled down, began to throb softly, and their vibration pulsed through the vessel. Slowly she began to move, and in the black darkness she slid away from her berth.

Sensei prayed silently, committing herself to God's care. Gradually the ship picked up speed, and the throb of the engines strengthened. At last Sensei slept.

When she woke the next morning, the ship was moving steadily. There was a measure of relief among the cabin mates, and Sensei learned that all five of the others were Jewish refugees fleeing from Hitler's Germany. Her heart went out to them.

The order came for them to report on deck for life-saving drill. Passengers, wearing their life jackets, hurried to obey.

Officers gave them quick, terse instructions and assigned them to lifeboats; Sensei found that she and a young missionary named Helen Morrisey enroute to the United States with twin babies and a little girl of three were assigned to the same boat.

She wasted no time making friends with the pretty young woman, and before breakfast was over, Sensei was helping with the babies and exchanging experiences with her new friends.

"One thing the Lord never gave me was twins!" Sensei beamed. "I always did wish He would!"

By afternoon Sensei was mothering the whole little family. They had just settled down in a sunny place on the deck, and Sensei had promised to tell the three-year-old a story, when the pleasant quiet was shattered by the muffled roar of an explosion. The ship lurched awkwardly and seemed to stagger.

"Torpedo!" The cry echoed through the ship.

Almost instantly the decks were a sea of confusion. Passengers, their faces twisted with shock and fear, rushed for their stations. Cries and shouts filled the air, and the voices of the officers, issuing orders, could be heard above them.

Sensei caught up the three-year-old. "We go this way!" she cried.

Helen Morrisey, clutching her babies in her arms, followed Sensei. Crewmen were rapidly helping passengers into the boats. Sensei passed the little girl to one of them and he lifted her in, and Sensei made sure that the mother and two babies were in the lifeboat before she got in. The little girl was crying; the mother, her arms already full, was trying to comfort her.

"Now you let me take the babies!" Sensei said. "I've had many to care for. They'll be fine with me."

Gratefully Mrs. Morrisey gave her the twins and gathered her frightened little daughter into her arms. The ship was listing more now. Life boats were being lowered away. With a lurch and a sickening swing, their boat went over the side, and Sensei whispered a prayer as the boat struck the water.

"Thank you, dear Lord, for making the sea calm," she prayed. "And for giving me twins at last to care for."

Seamen rowed the boat away from the listing vessel. All around the ship the small boats were hovering, looking as fragile as Japanese toys, Sensei thought, with the vastness of the ocean stretching all around them.

Aboard the ship, members of the crew worked frantically to repair the damage the German submarine had done. For hours the tense, frightened passengers huddled in the lifeboats. The babies in Sensei's arms began to fuss and cry, and then to squall in earnest.

"Sure, you're hungry," Sensei murmured, rocking them in her arms. But there was no food.

"Lord, what can I do?" Sensei thought. There seemed no answer. Shifting the babies to one arm, Sensei reached into the pocket of her coat to get her handkerchief. Her fingers touched a bottle of malted milk tablets! She pulled the bottle from her pocket and looked at it, her face shining.

"You never let me down, Lord!" she breathed. "You always answer every need!"

She took a tablet from the bottle and sucked it to soften it. Then she put one of the tablets into the baby's mouths. Its little face puckered up at first, and Sensei thought he was going to spit out the unaccustomed food. Then his eyes widened as though he had discovered something wonderful, and he began sucking at the softened tablet. Hurriedly Sensei softened another tablet for the other baby, and he, too, began to suck hungrily. For a while Sensei had her hands full, feeding first one baby and then the other.

It was late in the day when the ship's officers were finally satisfied that the vessel was seaworthy, and one by one the lifeboats were hoisted back on deck. Sensei, still holding the babies, bowed her head in a prayer of thanks, and Mrs. Morrisey and her little daughter prayed with her. All over the deck similar little groups were forming. Not a single life had been lost.

"But weren't you afraid?" Helen Morrisey asked her later. "I thought 'If the ship goes down we will all die here,' and I was terrified. But you—seemed to be calm."

Sensei looked at her through her thick glasses. She smiled gently. "A long time ago," she said, "I read a verse from Proverbs: 'As thou goest step by step, I will open up thy way before thee.' " She paused a moment. "The lifeboats were just a step," she said. "And if the next step were to Him, the way was open and prepared."

A look of wonder came into the younger missionary's face. "What a wonderful verse," she whispered. "I will never forget it!"

It took the disabled ship twenty–three days to reach New York. The course was slow and difficult, and there were many hardships aboard. But among the passengers there was a feeling of faith which was almost tangible. Perhaps it was their miraculous escape there in the ocean that made this. And perhaps it was Sensei's presence that made it evident.

Sensei had only a few hours in New York and only time for

the briefest reunion with her brother and his family. She thought longingly of the nearness of New Jersey and wished that she might at least see Al for just a few minutes, but there had been no chance to notify him of her coming, and a telephone call to his bachelor rooms got no answer.

With a small sigh in her heart, she boarded the train that took her on the long cross-country jouney. But as the train sped across the States, the feeling of urgency to be back in Japan grew in her again. It became so strong that she found herself willing the train to go faster.

"Lord," she asked silently, "what is it that hastens me?" But there was no reply.

Reaching Vancouver at last, she stayed overnight with the Vernors, and to her delight they had Canadian salmon, exactly as they had had that first time she was a guest in their home. The picture with the verse she trusted so still hung in the bedroom where she and Adelaide had stayed, and she was deeply glad.

"It's like a sign," she told her old friends.

But the steps she was taking on this journey seemed to be frought with danger. First there had been the torpedoing in the Atlantic. And now as the ship neared Yokohama after its journey across the Pacific, a violent typhoon struck. For four days the ship wallowed and rolled in the angry sea while wind and rain lashed at it. So great was the force of the wind that it could make no progress. Passengers scarcely dared move from their cabins, and Sensei, praying for the safety of all, asked:

"Lord, what is it? Do these dangers mean that You do not want me to return to Japan? Have I misread your directives?"

Instantly, that same strong feeling of urgency rushed over

her, and she heard herself saying out loud: "I must go! I must go!" She felt bewildered, and she prayed earnestly through the last hours of the storm asking God to instruct her, but the message He had for her was not yet to be known.

When the storm had finally abated, the battered liner limped into port and the weary passengers disembarked. Sensei had hoped that Mercy and some of her "Sunbeams" might be at the dock to meet her, or perhaps even Adelaide who during her year's absence had been transferred to Suma, not far from Akashi, where she was serving in a JEB Girls' Bible College; but no one was there, not even Jim Cuthbertson, the field director.

"I'm getting to be too much of an old stand-by," Sensei chuckled to herself. Still, she was more than eager to get to Sunrise Home.

She traveled to Tokyo, and the strange feeling of abandonment she had had on disembarking seemed to come closer. There was something—something that was wrong. Something in the air. She looked about at the familiar sights, the faces of the people. They seemed the same. But they weren't. Not quite. There was something different.

In Tokyo she was questioned by the Japanese secret police before she could board the train to Akashi. She was genuinely astonished.

"But everyone knows me and my work!" she exclaimed. "I'm Smith Sensei!"

They were polite, but they were stiff, and Sensei felt the worry growing within her. Still as she neared the town which she loved so well, her spirits lifted. The sight of the familiar bit of the Inland Sea made her feel deeply welcome, and the scent of the pines as she came toward her new and gracious Sunrise

Home filled her heart with the glory of God.

She had not wired from Tokyo, so her coming was a surprise, and all of the children, little and big, welcomed her with cries and hugs and such love that her Irish heart melted. Mercy and Oka-san were overjoyed, too, yet in their faces she saw something which was not reflected in the children's. There was a shadow in them.

As soon as she could, she drew Mercy aside. "What is it?" she asked simply.

"It is the war in Europe," Mercy said, her voice betraying her inner anxiety. "Things aren't the same here, Irene. The military party is in control of the country. We are not as welcome here as we were. I'm afraid we are not wanted."

Sensei stared at her in disbelief. "Now how is that possible?" she asked. "We bring only love."

Mercy shook her head. "I know," she said. "But be prepared for—changes."

Sensei could not accept at that moment the idea that things could be changed. Perhaps a few things—a few rules and regulations, such as questioning by the secret police. But underneath —basically—things must be the same.

She set about her work with vigor and happiness, but slowly and gradually the changes Mercy had mentioned began to come home to her. She could not travel to Tokyo without being questioned, and sometimes at length. What was she doing here? Why was she in the country? Who was she working for?

"But you know all these answers!" she cried. "I am here to care for my children!"

A short, stocky Japanese with heavy eyebrows sneered at her. "They are not yours!" he said. And Sensei felt a stab of fear.

She sought out the Mikis, her old friends, and Dr. Saiki. They were genuinely glad to see her, and she knew that their faith burned as brightly as it ever had, but she saw anxiety in their faces, too.

"There is a strong feeling against foreigners now," Mr. Miki said sadly. "There is hate in the air."

Sensei slipped to her knees. Mr. Miki and his wife joined her, and they prayed together. When they rose at last, there were tears in Mr. Miki's eyes. "We pray every day," he said simply. "There are many of us who pray every day that this feeling will be wiped out."

At JEB headquarters there was worry, too, and Adelaide, when she saw her, shook her head. But Sensei still struggled, praying nightly for guidance.

She found it increasingly difficult to manage the Home. Some of the supplies from England never were delivered. And in the faces of the children she began to see some unspoken doubts and questionings. She tried to still them.

Then word came from the British Ambassador: Foreigners were to conclude their affairs in Japan and withdraw.

Sensei was motionless with shock. She stared blankly about her—at the rooms, at the furnishings, at the grove of pines seen through the windows. In the yard she could hear the shouts of the children at play, and she thought of the older ones, gathered in their rooms, talking and chattering, planning ahead to the time of their high school graduations, and maybe jobs, and some day their own homes.

"Oh, my God!" Sensei whispered. "What step is this that Thou dost lead me to?"

An unmistakable conviction came over her which she could not ignore—the long-awaited answer to her question:

You must find homes for your children, Sensei!

Then the tears streamed down Sensei's cheeks and she lifted her heart to the Lord. "This is why I was called back!" she whispered. "This is the urgency I felt! I had to come here quickly so that my little ones wouldn't be seized—so that each one of them would be placed in a good Christian home!"

Alone that night Sensei prayed. By morning she had found the courage. She was calm and serene at morning prayers, and she gathered her "family" about her. It had changed over the years. The old couple who had come to them that night at Akashi had gone Home. Some of the older girls had married, some were working. But those who surrounded her were still her "family."

In steady tones, Sensei told them that Sunrise Home must now be closed. The children stared at her uncomprehendingly, even the oldest ones unable to take it all in.

"But don't you love us any more?" Akiko burst out.

Sensei gathered the child into her arms. "I love you, and the Lord loves you!" she said, and for a moment she buried her face against the child's soft hair. When she looked up, there was only assurance in her face, and it reached out to the children.

"Remember that I have always taught you that the Lord leads you step by step," she said. "And He leads us now. He will help me find a good home for each one of you! A home where you'll be loved."

But the children could not take this in. All they knew was that they loved Sensei and she loved them, and that now their beloved Sensei and the only Home they knew were being taken away from them. They pressed about Sensei, begging her to stay, saying they would be good children.

"That I know," Sensei said softly. "But when our Lord bids us to be brave, we must not fail Him."

Sensei spent the next day in prayer alone. In the hours she spent before the Lord, she first confessed her sense of loneliness at the thought of leaving her children.

"You have guided my steps through the years, Lord. I can't doubt You now. I'm sure You have homes for every one of these precious little girls. I pray that they will find loving homes—Christian homes where they will be wanted. And, Lord, take the sting of parting from all of our hearts."

The next day was Wednesday. Sensei suddenly realized that the Christians would be meeting that evening for prayer in the little church at Akashi. She decided she would ask her Japanese brothers and sisters in Christ to share her heavy burden. It was proper and fitting that she seek their fellowship in requesting the Lord to perform the miracle of providing homes for forty-eight little girls who were still with her.

Sensei bustled off to the church and arrived just as the small group of believers were gathering for the service. She told the pastor she had an urgent prayer request. Then she told the congregation of the need to close the home unless, perchance, the Japanese themselves could carry on the work. Then she sat down and quietly waited.

One after another, the Akashi Christians prayed. There was fervency and feeling in every petition, and a growing sense of expectancy as the meeting proceeded.

"Lord, I know You hear our cries," Sensei spoke out, almost forgetting where she was.

Near the end of the service, Mr. Miki, who was one of the church elders, arose and addressed himself to the Irish missionary who had meant so much to him and his loved ones:

"Sensei, we are so grateful to God for sending you here, for the way He has used you to lead us and our families to Jesus

Christ. We wish we could be of help to you at this time. But we realize that we could never take over that big Sunrise Home. We don't have the people for the job and there will be no funds coming from abroad. It looks like you will have to dispose of the property."

Then he paused and smiled warmly at Sensei: "But we have thought of a way of helping you. The Lord has been speaking to us in this meeting. We are willing to take the children into our homes. I am sure there will be Christians from other churches who will join us in this. *We'll care for the children until you come back again.*"

Sensei began to weep, but with a sense of joy and gratitude for the warm response of the Japanese Christians. She recognized that again the Lord was preparing the way before her. She knew how rare adoptions were in Japan, and she was certain that God had been working in the hearts of His people.

After the service Sensei was besieged with requests for children. The next day the Christian families from all over the region eagerly besought Sensei to turn her little charges over to their keeping.

But she decided she would keep the children with her until the moment of her departure. Besides, she wanted each child to have a brand-new outfit and her entire wardrobe in shape before going to her new home. With the help of Oka San and the Sunrise staff, Sensei launched a huge sewing project. Working like beavers, the crew headed by Oka San checked every little girl's clothing, inspecting dresses, darning stockings, repairing, washing, and pressing everything in sight.

In the busy days that followed, Sensei interviewed prospective foster parents, discussed the developments with the children themselves, and soon realized that nearly every child had been placed. Indeed there were far more offers of homes than there were children!

Only Hanachan, who had come to the Home so long ago, a tiny, sickly baby unwanted by anyone, was left. Now she was a beautiful girl of seventeen. It was obvious that Hanachan was concerned because no family had sought to adopt her. Finally one evening after prayers, she looked up soberly into Sensei's face.

"I'm too old, am I not?" she asked.

Sensei's heart twisted. The child had spoken the very thing that Sensei had begun to fear herself. She had tried desperately to find a place for this little girl who was very dear to her, but she had had no success at all, and time was getting short.

"There will be someone, child," Sensei said, and Mercy put her hand on Hanachan's shoulder reassuringly.

Hanachan shook her head. "I don't think so," she said. "I have been thinking about it a long time, and I know you must go. I know you had another notice from the Ambassador just the other day, and he wants you to leave." She looked deeply into Sensei's face as if she were studying every line. She didn't see the gray hair, or the wrinkles that had come, or the thick glasses. She saw love, and she gave it back from a full heart. "I want you to go now," she said. "I will manage by myself. I have already gone to see some people about work. The telephone company thinks they may have a place for me."

Sensei took heart. She caught Hanachan's hands in hers and held them tight. Though years had passed since she first came to Japan, and though many things had changed, she knew how hard it still was for a young girl alone to make a living, and she knew where many of them who were defenseless were forced.

"There will be a place," she said strongly. "Have faith, Hana."

That night Sensei talked soberly to Mercy. It was true what Hanachan said—finding a place for a seventeen-year-old just didn't seem possible.

"I have been thinking," Sensei said slowly. "Tomorrow I am going to Tokyo. I'm going to see if I can't get permission to take Hanachan with me when I leave."

Mercy's face looked tired. "Oh, my dear," she said. "How could you manage?"

"With the Lord's help!" Sensei said stoutly.

The next day she went to Tokyo. It was hard to get around. The streets seemed to be teeming with people, and everything was noisy and crowded. Sensei was pushed and shoved, and the whole atmosphere of the city made her bone tired. She started her round of the government offices, trudging from one to another in the hope that someone might have mercy in his heart. But everywhere the answer was the same:

"No, it is impossible. No Japanese national is allowed to leave the country."

At last even Sensei was defeated, and she took the late train back to Akashi. She had not told Hanachan what her errand had been. She did not need to tell Mercy what the results of it had been. Her face showed it.

Tired, as she was, Sensei could not sleep. Finally she got up and, pulling her warmest dressing gown around her, went outside. It was bright moonlight, and the whole countryside was bathed in beauty. Sensei walked slowly, not paying attention to where she was going, and suddenly she found herself at the well. She stood there looking at it, and memory flooded through her. Only she had had faith that water would be found then. The well diggers, the experts—all had told her she was wrong. But the Lord had shown His faithfulness.

She got to her knees, more slowly now than she had in those earlier days, and she bowed her head.

"Lord, I believe that Thou art able," she prayed. "I have faith as a grain of mustard seed, such as the faith of the little ones whose faith moved their mountain. Help me. Provide a home for Hanachan. . . . if You will."

For a long time she stayed there in meditation, and when she went back to her room, she fell at once into a sweet sleep.

She was packing some of the last belongings which were to be sent to an orphanage the next morning, when a knock came at the door. Mercy was busy upstairs, and Hanachan in the kitchen, so Sensei went to the door herself. A pleasant-faced Japanese woman and her husband stood there. The man had the appearance of a successful businessman.

They bowed and exchanged formal greeting, and then the woman spoke in English. "We have heard that you are giving children for adoption," she said. "That is why we came."

"I'm sorry," Sensei said. "All the babies have been taken."

The woman explained that she and her husband had come to Japan from Korea on a business trip, and that he had appointments later in the morning. "Would you let me stay here while he's busy in Osaka?" she asked.

"Of course you're welcome," Sensei said warmly. "But you will have to make yourself at home. We are making the final preparations for leaving the Home, and I am afraid I am that busy!"

The husband took his leave, saying he would be back late in the afternoon. The woman offered to help, and sensing that there was something on her mind and that working might help her, Sensei let her assist with the packing. They worked side by side for a while, making only the ordinary polite conversation, and then the woman's story began to come out.

"My husband and I are Christians," she said, and then added: "But we have had some difficult experiences."

Sensei nodded without speaking. She had long since learned that when someone wanted to unburden herself the kindest way to help them was often not to ask questions.

"We had a child," the woman went on after a pause. "A little girl—she would be seventeen now. She was stricken with polio a year ago, and we could not save her."

Sensei murmured a word of compassion.

"I wanted to kill myself then. The only thing that stopped me was love for my husband. But all of the faith I'd had left me. I kept asking, 'Why did God do this to me? Why did He take my child? Couldn't He have taken some other child—a child from a big family?' "

The woman went on to tell Sensei that she made up her mind she would never enter a church again, never open her Bible, never have any trust in God.

"I decided to go my own way," she said. "I refused to see our pastor or the Bible women from our church. I had the outside shutters closed and ordered the servants to say I was not at home."

Sensei folded another small baby garment and put it in the box, all the while listening intently.

"After a while I became ill," the woman said. "I stayed in bed for days. I had no interest, even in my husband, and finally he stayed away from our home as much as he could."

She told how this went on for months, while she grew more and more wretched. And then one day when one servant had gone shopping and another was hanging out the laundry, she heard the postman's cry: *"Yubin!"* and heard the thud of a package in the hallway.

More for lack of something to do than anything else, she went and picked up the package and carried it back to bed with her. It was from somewhere in Japan, and it was addressed to her. Curious, she opened it.

"I found that it was a book about a Japanese girl named Kazue," she said, and Sensei's head came up sharply. "Before I realized what I was doing, I began to read the book, and before I had turned a page, I came on the name of Jesus Christ.

"Everything in me revolted. I threw the book across the room. But I couldn't get the book out of my mind. I got up and got the book and started to read again. And again I threw it away from me. This happened several times. But finally I read the book to the end."

The woman stopped, her hands folded quietly in her lap, and Sensei waited. Then the woman looked straight at Sensei. "I knelt by my bed and asked God to forgive me," she said. "I don't know how long I was there, but it was a long time, and I felt all the bitterness taken from me.

"I got up then, and bathed, and dressed myself in my best kimono. I went to the garden and cut some flowers, and then to the kitchen to see about the evening meal.

"When my husband came home, he could scarcely believe that I was up and dressed—and grateful to see him home."

She told how she had asked her husband to read Kazue's book, too, and how they had talked about it, and then had thanked God together for His goodness.

"We don't know who sent the book," she said. "It was like a gift from God."

"It was," Sensei said softly.

The woman told her that her husband had been planning a business trip to Japan and had previously asked her to go with him, but she had refused. Now she asked him to take her, and he agreed gladly.

"I want to visit Akashi, I told him," the woman concluded. "I want to see Sunrise Home and the things Kazue wrote of. I want to meet that Sensei!"

Sensei laughed, her eyes a little misty. "And I think God sent you," she said. Then she told her that, although there were no babies left, there was a lovely seventeen-year-old girl who needed a home. She told her of Hanachan.

The woman drew back abruptly, shaking her head. "No!" she said tightly. "We could not take a girl that age. No one can replace our daughter. It is better to begin over with a little child."

Sensei tried to talk to her. The woman remained adamant, but in Sensei's mind was a plan, and in her heart a singing faith. Surely this was the answer the Lord had sent her!

She had to go on with her duties, and she left the woman to wander about the grounds as she pleased. Sensei slipped down to the kitchen.

"See that we have a very *special* tea today, Hana," she said. "We are entertaining the last guests we will have here at Sunrise Home."

Late in the afternoon, the woman's husband returned, and Sensei invited them to tea. Mercy joined them, and Hanachan, dressed in a pretty kimono, served them. Her every move was graceful. Her manners flawless. The woman couldn't take her eyes off her, and when the tea was finished and Hanachan had withdrawn, she said:

"She is the image of our daughter!"

Even Sensei was startled.

The husband nodded, agreeing with his wife, and suddenly the woman reached across and put her hand tightly on Sensei's arm.

"May we have her?" she asked. "May we take her back to Korea with us?"

Sensei's heart overflowed, and she was as near tears as she had ever been. She told the woman how hard they had tried to place Hanachan, and how she had been sure the Lord would answer her prayers.

"And He sent you," she said. "His ways are miraculous!"

The miracle was not quite complete yet. For when the records required for adoption were checked, it was found that Hanachan had been born on the *same day, the same month, the same year* as the daughter the couple had lost!

Now only Mercy and Sensei were left. There was only one thing more to do: dispose of the property. Sensei's heart was heavy as she began to look for someone to take it over. She could not bear to have the Home go to just anyone, and she searched diligently for a possible buyer who might love the Home as she had.

Adelaide, looking worn and thin, came from Suma to stay until time of departure. The three women, whose lives had been so full, whose days so busy, found themselves in strange idleness.

At last Sensei found a renter for the Home—the officials of the Kobe Christian Orphanage who were in desperate need of more space.

"Oh, praise God!" Sensei told the others that night. "There

will be children here, and Sunrise Home will continue to be used in the Lord's service."

She accepted a modest rental payment in advance and penned an informal paper turning over the property to the Orphanage. She signed it, *Su misu*—the Japanese characters for Smith.

The final details completed, the last of the belongings packed, Adelaide and Sensei said their last good-bys to the Home and the land and the people they had loved, and on December 23, 1940, they sailed from Yokohama on the *Hikawa Maru*. No one of them knew what the future might hold.

12

Search for Her Girls

The *Hikawa Maru* ploughed eastward through the Pacific waters. Sensei, walking the deck with Adelaide or sitting beside her in their deck chairs, felt tired and alone. Thoughts of her children, now scattered throughout Japan, tugged at her, and the knowledge that she would never again walk through the rooms of Sunrise Home or pause for a moment to be refreshed by a glimpse of the Inland Sea made her feel that the chapter in her life which had begun so many years ago was over. All of her adult life had been given to active service to God, and the feeling that she would now step from such work grew stronger within her.

Her thoughts drifted to Al, and there was both nostalgia and longing in them. Perhaps the time had come when at last they would have a life together, quiet and good.

She stirred, thinking how blessed it would be, the fellowship they would have, the joy of a home warmed by their affection.

Was it too late for that? She bit her lip, thinking. "I'm fifty-three," she said, not knowing she'd spoken aloud.

Adelaide gave her a sharp look. "Of course you are," she said crisply. "What of it?"

Sensei smiled a little. "Nothing," she said, "I was only thinking."

Misreading her thoughts, Adelaide sat a little straighter. "We're not too old to start over," she said. "There's no good thinking how straitened our circumstances are. The Lord will help us."

Sensei blinked. She had certainly not been thinking about finances! But she had to admit they were something to be reckoned with. They had no source of income. It was impossible to get money out of England.

"Well!" Sensei said, her voice astonished. "I never thought of *that!*"

"It's something to think of," Adelaide said dryly.

"Sensei chuckled. "You've just answered that yourself," she said. "The Lord will provide."

They landed in Vancouver on a Saturday night. The Vernor sisters met them, glad as always to see them, but fretting because they would not be able to have them as guests in their home. Every inch of space was already occupied by JEB missionaries who, like Sensei and Adelaide, had been ordered from their posts.

"We've found rooms for you though," they said. "Just opposite the Fairfield Presbyterian Church. They already want you to speak there. I'm sure you'll be in great demand for meetings!"

Sensei slanted a look at Adelaide, as much as to say: *You see?* and the two of them went along with their friends to their new quarters. The Vernors insisted they have dinner with them that night, and there was a glad reunion with old friends—as well as the delicious dinner Sensei always looked forward to!

Adelaide and Sensei plunged into a round of lectures and meetings, and it was very soon evident that Sensei communicated extraordinarily well with the young people. Attendance at the youth meeting grew, and interest was always high.

One of those who heard her speak was a man in charge of the Inter-Varsity Christian Fellowship, an interdenominational fellowship in the Pacific Northwest. He was extremely impressed with her ability to get the attention of young people, and he contacted Stacey Woods, the founder and general secretary of the IVCF, recommending that Sensei be considered as a staff worker. Woods listened to her message and promptly asked her to serve with the Fellowship.

"I don't know," Sensei said to Adelaide. "It's not anything I'd ever thought of before. I can't seem to decide."

"You will when the time comes," Adelaide said with her usual decisiveness. She turned away then and walked to the window, where she stood looking out for a moment. Then she turned back to Sensei. "I have made my decision, Irene," she said. "I've prayed over it many nights now, and I feel I know what the Lord's will is for me."

She went on to say that she had decided to return to her home in England. Her sister was ill, and wartime conditions made it even more difficult for her. "I feel my place is with her," Adelaide concluded. "I am leaving tomorrow for New York."

Sensei felt the words jolt against her. She and Adelaide had been together so many years! It was like another part of her life being torn away, and her thoughts flashed again to Al and the comfort there would be in sharing life with him. But she pushed her personal thoughts away and took Adelaide's hands in hers.

"You know how I will miss you," she said. "Godspeed, Adelaide, and my heart goes with you."

She saw Adelaide off the next morning, and she would not admit even to herself how lonely she felt as the train pulled away from the station. An intense longing to go to the nearest telephone and put in a long distance call to Al came over her, and she half turned in search of a booth. But she stopped herself.

"Not yet," she said. "Not when it's my loneliness making me reach toward him."

She plunged into work, speaking all over the Northwest wherever she was called, putting off Stacey Woods who continued to press her to become a staff member of the IVCF.

On December 7, 1941, the Japanese planes bombed Pearl Harbor. Sensei was stunned by the news. She broke off an appointment for a lecture and went to her room where she stayed alone, praying. Her heart was heavy—heavier than she had ever known it to be as the shadow of war reached out across the world.

It was not long before Sensei found new work. In the United States the Nisei were being moved into internment camps as a security measure, and Sensei's heart was touched. Even though she was told the harsh moves were necessary, she could not help but think of the people torn from their homes, moved into barracks, fenced in by barbed wire; and she knew that they needed spiritual counsel. Once again she felt the call of God, and instead of the letter she had thought of writing to Al, she wrote instead: "My work is not yet done. I feel I must stay on for I am so needed by these people. But, dear friend, I hope that this war will be over soon, and that we may meet again, for I am longing to see you. I remember so dearly those days of long ago, and I will tell you now I have a wish to be reunited with you. Pray that the war will soon be ended."

She sent the letter off on a beautiful spring day in April. Three days later she received a telegram. Al had died of pneumonia.

The telegram shook in Sensei's hand. Dizziness swept over her, and she closed her eyes against it, putting out a hand to the back of a chair to steady herself. "Oh, no!" she whispered. "Oh, no!"

Slow tears slid down her face, and grief ached in her heart. She slipped to her knees beside her bed and buried her face against her arms. She wept then—alone and lonely, and with tears on her cheeks she prayed.

The hands of the clock moved inexorably forward, and Irene closed her grief away. In the Nisei camp people were waiting for her, and their needs came first. With one last prayer, she rose, steadying herself, and then she made herself ready and went to those who waited the consolation of the words which she would bring them.

Not long after Al's death, Sensei, after deep consultation with her Lord, accepted a staff position with IVCF on a temporary basis. She was sent to fill the post of chaplain at Pioneer Girls' Camp in the Muskoka Region of Ontario, and in her mind she pictured it as something like Sunrise Home.

She was thoroughly bewildered when she arrived. The camp teemed with activities. The girls ran around in shorts and slacks which to her Victorian mind steeped in Japanese culture was completely outlandish. The accent was on sports, and Sensei, whatever else she might be was not a sportswoman in spite of her tomboy youth, and she felt completely at sea.

She found that not being able to paddle a canoe meant a considerable loss of status, and she determined to learn—and by herself, too! Night after night when quiet settled over the camp after everyone had gone to bed, Sensei, tucking up her skirt, crept from her bunk and headed for the canoe shelter. As noiselessly as she could she launched a canoe awkwardly into the water and managed to get aboard. With typical Sensei determination she gave herself lessons in paddling until she could handle a canoe with considerable aplomb, and she kept her silence when the young campers chattered about "a phantom paddler" on the lake every night.

When she was confident enough, she surprised everyone one day by striding down to the lake in broad daylight, getting into a canoe as though there were nothing to it, and paddling off across the lake. The girls cheered; Sensei confessed; the mystery of the midnight paddler was solved.

Sensei was soon a favorite at the camp. She regaled the girls with stories of Japan when they sat around the campfire at night. One of the girls wrote a poem about her:

> "No one tells tales as Sensei can
> Of things that happened in Japan,
> And every day we seem to hear:
> 'But that's another story dear.' "

So successful was Sensei with her IVCF assignments that Woods sent her to work on campuses on the west coast of the United States. War restrictions made traveling difficult, but

Sensei always managed to get from campus to campus, and wherever she went she helped establish IVCF chapters.

If sometimes at night she felt tired and lonely, if sometimes her thoughts turned to Al or to Adelaide or the children of Sunrise Home, she never let anyone know. She went staunchly on about her work, trying to reach others for Jesus Christ.

In the summer of 1943, with the war raging around the world, Sensei was requested to help set up a new Inter-Varsity camp in Ontario's Lake of the Bays. It was a rugged summer for the aging missionary. The embryonic camp was primitive, to say the least. Sensei slept on a double-deck bed with no mattress, washed in cold water, and fought off insects. While the men hammered away building cabins, Sensei spent hours sewing curtains and bedspreads, scouring fire-blackened pans and even occasionally helping to drive nails. At last the job was over; and the night it was completed, Sensei, older in years than any of them, but young in spirit, broke into a wild Irish jig of celebration.

From the woods of Canada she was sent to the State College for Women in Denton, Texas. Authorities were reluctant to have her speak on campus at first, but after her initial speech she was invited to live on campus. She soon establised noon prayer meetings and conducted prayer meetings in the dormitories. Her presence changed the entire tone of the college.

She was invited one evening to have dinner with the president of the college and his wife, and after the meal, the two women retired to the sitting room for a chat. The president's wife confided that she feared she had cancer and asked Sensei to pray for her. Sensei did this, and then talked with the woman about Christ's claims. Before they parted, another soul had been won for the Savior.

On the same campus there was a rebellious girl who had been a constant problem to the authorities. Though the girls were requested to dress for dinner, the rebel wore an old hat, slacks, and a dirty coat. She glowered at everyone, and her only pleasure seemed to be in breaking the rules.

One night when Sensei was addressing a meeting, the girl came in late, banging the door and clumping loudly across the room to a seat. Sensei was telling the students that when the Lord Jesus Christ took charge of a person, He changed one's whole life and demeanor.

The rebel scowled at her and sat slouched in her seat when the others left. Sensei started up the stairs to her room. Suddenly there was a clatter behind her, and the girl shouted Sensei's name. Sensei turned, waiting for her.

"What do you mean," the girl demanded belligerently, "about a changed life?"

"Why don't you come up to my room and we'll talk about it?" Sensei asked.

The girl agreed, and before Sensei began her talk she tried to draw the girl out. Soon the unhappy girl was pouring out her whole story. She was the child of a broken home and had been shunted about for most of her young life. She felt that nobody wanted her, and as a result she tried to hate everyone so she couldn't be hurt.

Quietly Sensei began to talk about Jesus, and bit by bit explained how life could take on new meaning. The young girl broke down and wept, sobbing that she wanted a new life, that the unhappiness of her old one was almost more than she could bear. Before she left she confessed faith in Christ.

There was a radical and joyous change in the girl's behavior after that. Her rude manners ceased. Her seeming hatred of others vanished. She became a bright witness for Christ.

The years rolled on. D-Day came and passed, and Sensei thanked God that at least part of the holocaust was over. She prayed that peace would come soon.

In the summer of 1945 she found herself at the IVCF camp in Canada again, now a beautiful and thriving Campus of the Woods.

She sat with others of the staff and with a group of students listening to the radio one day in early August when the program was suddenly interrupted. There in the peace of the Canadian woods they heard that an atomic bomb had been dropped on Hiroshima. Two days later came news of the bombing of Nagasaki. The news was shocking. It could scarcely be taken in. Sensei was so shaken that she withdrew to her room, there to pray hour after hour. "O Lord, bring us peace," she prayed. "Bring us peace."

On August 14, the news of Japan's surrender reached the camp. For the second time in her life, Sensei wept unashamedly. This time it was from thankfulness.

The end of the war brought abrupt changes to Sensei's life. Her one wish was to return to Japan. Because she traveled on a British passport, it was necessary for her first to return to London. There she was told that it would be at least *six months* before she could hope to get a permit to go to Japan. "It will be a miracle if you even get it then," said Tommy, a young man she recognized from the British Embassy in Tokyo.

"Tommy, your idea of miracles and mine are two different things. If you get me a permit in six *weeks,* that's a miracle."

He took her registration card and flipped it into the air, saying "I won't need this for a while."

But Sensei was confident. "Here is my telephone number," she added "I will expect to hear from you in a few days."

The clerk smiled condescendingly, but a few days later when he called Sensei as she had expected, all the condescension was gone. Sensei's permit had arrived.

Though Sensei did not know it until later, what had happened was this: When General Douglas MacArthur took over the occupation government of Japan, he sought to develop every means of restoring the Japanese nation. One thing he did was send out a call for experienced missionaries who spoke the Japanese language. The proclamation was announced over the radio, and Sensei's old friend, Dr. Saiki, heard it. He immediately wrote to General MacArthur urging him to try to locate Irene Webster-Smith and saying that they would be glad to have her share their home with them if she came back to Japan.

The General at once contacted London, and his call for Miss Webster-Smith's services came only a few days after Sensei had requested travel permission.

"It's all God's providential arranging," she said with certainty when she heard the story.

After a very rough passage, Sensei disembarked at Kure, her heart eager for reunion with old friends, bursting with the hope of somehow finding and seeing each one of her former "Sunbeams."

Her papers were inspected by both a British and an American officer, who seemed extremely suspicious about her permit and questioned her closely about it.

"What is wrong with it?" Sensei asked.

"We've never seen one like it," they told her.

Sensei told them her story, and they looked at her wonderingly. "Everyone else arriving at this port is restricted to a ten-mile radius of Kure!" they said. "Your permit says you can go anywhere in Japan!"

The first place she went was to Kyoto where the Saikis lived. She was saddened by the sights of the ravages of war, and when she reached the Saiki home she felt new shock. Dr. Saiki looked thin and worn. His wife had died. The lovely old home was in a state of disrepair. All the members of the family slept on the first floor, for the leaking roof made the upper floors uninhabitable. Food was scarce, and there was an air of poverty everywhere.

Sensei's heart was heavy. If the Saikis who had been so prosperous had fared so poorly, what had happened to other friends?

Still, she was greeted warmly and made welcome by the doctor and his children, who more than willingly shared what little they had with her. Unwilling to cause them more deprivation, Sensei found a room at the YWCA as soon as she could, but she had real concern for her friends.

Invited by an Australian colonel to have lunch, Sensei accepted with alacrity. Soup, meat, vegetables, bread and butter, tea and dessert were served—a royal repast in Japan those days.

"I haven't had this much food since I've been here," Sensei told the Colonel candidly.

"I was going to apologize for the poor meal," he said. "What do you live on?"

"Japanese rations," she said. "If we are fortunate, we get three small bowls of rice a week. Sometimes we get potatoes and American corn meal. We have no sugar, no salt, and no fat of any kind."

The Colonel was more than concerned. He insisted on giving Sensei a large quantity of rations and insisted on writing to

Australia to get permission for her to buy food from the commissary.

At first Sensei was tempted to refuse. She felt morally that she should share the hardships of the people whom she served, and that doing so would be evidence of her sincerity and friendship. But then she thought of the Saikis and of all the others who were going hungry. Surely the Lord would not mind if she bought what she could and shared it with others. Was this not His provision for them? What she could buy would be no more than a trickle in the midst of great need, yet it was something. Primly Sensei accepted the Colonel's offer.

The men in the commissary loaded a jeep with canned milk, tea, flour, shortening, cooking oil, tins of meat, fruit and vegetables and other provisions—the Colonel's gift. Sensei had the driver go straight to the Saikis. She bustled ahead of the men as they started carrying in the boxes, and the whole Saiki family gathered around, almost unable to believe their eyes.

"Where did you get all this?" Dr. Saiki asked when the men had gone, tears in his eyes.

"They're the Lord's provisions," Sensei said. After that, with every cent she could get together, Sensei bought "provisions from the Lord" and distributed them to others.

She had been kept extremely busy her first few weeks in Japan and had had only time to make random inquiries about the whereabouts of her former charges, and the longing to see them was almost overwhelming. For the seven years she had been gone, each one of them had stayed in her mind, and she had ached for news of them. But there had been no way to hear of them in those days. Now back in her adopted land, she could wait no longer.

She began her search. Through Dr. Saiki she located the first girl—Micheko, who was now working as a trained nurse in Doshisha University Hospital in Kyoto. Bursting with excitement, Sensei hurried there, and as she came onto the ward, Micheko rushed into her arms.

"Oh, my Sensei! My Sensei!" she cried, and Sensei held her close. Both of them were crying. Then they were laughing and crying and trying to talk all at once.

Eagerly Micheko poured out what little news she had of the other girls, and Sensei plied her with questions, jotting down the few addresses Micheko had.

Micheko's face sobered. "You must see Noriko first," she said, and told Sensei that she was in the TB ward of the hospital and did not have long to live.

"When she was brought here," Micheko said, "she looked up at me and said, 'I won't die until Sensei gets back.' " Micheko shook her head. "We did not think she could live," she said. "But she has clung to life, and every day she has insisted that you would return. She has great faith—even as a little child—Sensei."

Micheko led her to the tuberculosis ward. "She's in the fifth bed to the right," she whispered. "Go in alone, Sensei. This time with you should be all hers."

Sensei went down the aisle between the beds, and she felt her heart squeeze with pain as she saw Noriko. Her face was waxen, her body wasted away. She lay motionless with her eyes closed.

Sensei stopped beside her and whispered her name. Noriko's eyes fluttered open, and a look of wonder and then joy filled them.

"Sensei!" she whispered, holding out her arms very much as she had when she was a small child. "I knew you'd come, Sensei!"

Sensei gathered her into her arms and rocked her like a baby. She felt new shock as she realized how shabby Noriko's nightclothes and bedlinen were—even soiled. She realized that there had been no soap and no supplies, and she thought how difficult this must have been for the Japanese who were always fastidious.

She smoothed Noriko's hair and talked to her softly. She dared not stay long, for Noriko was too weak; but she promised to return the next day, and when she did, she carried with her two clean sheets from the small store she had brought from Ireland and one of her own gowns and a bar of sweet smelling soap—the last one she had.

She herself bathed Noriko and slipped on the gown, so much too large for the thin, wasted body, and changed the bed linen.

Sighing, Noriko lay back. "I knew you'd come," she whispered again. "I knew you'd tidy me up before I went to Heaven."

Noriko was hungry for news of the other girls, but Sensei had none to give. But that night Dr. Saiki came to her to take her to the hospital again. A new patient had just been brought in, and this time it was Yoshichan.

Sensei couldn't suppress a cry. "Yoshichan!" she gasped. "She was Noriko's best friend! And now they both lie there in the same hospital." She looked anxiously at Dr. Saiki. "Is she as ill as my little Noriko?"

The doctor nodded soberly. "Hers is a sad story, Sensei," he said. "Her husband brought her to the hospital tonight and left her. He will not be back."

"Not be back!" Sensei cried. "What do you mean?"

"It's an old story to us," the doctor said wearily.

"A tragedy that has befallen many of our women who have

been stricken with tuberculosis. When they grow too ill, their husbands bring them to us and abandon them. Then they take a new wife who is young and pretty."

"Merciful God!" Sensei whispered. "What has the world come to?"

Putting her own sorrow away from her, Sensei accompanied the doctor back to the hospital, taking from her meager supplies what she had to offer. Yoshichan wept when she saw Sensei, and Sensei's heart wept for her. In broken tones Yoshichan told Sensei her story—the happiness she had known at first, the war, her husband's rejection of the Christianity he had professed. And last, in a whisper so low Sensei could barely hear it:

"I have a baby," she said, her eyes dark with grief. "A sweet baby, Sensei . . . He has taken her, too . . . I know I'll never see her."

Staunch as Sensei was, she could barely keep her emotions in control. She soothed Yoshichan, and ministered to her, and sought for some way to bring at least a small ray of happiness into Yoshichan's last days.

Murmuring to Yoshichan that she would be back, she sought out Dr. Saiki. "You must help me," she said without preamble. She told him Yoshiko's story. "Yoshichan and Noriko and Micheko, three of my little ones, are all here in this hospital," she finished, "but they are not together, and they must be! You must arrange it!"

It was not easy in the crowded, under-staffed hospital to make any changes, but Dr. Saiki managed it. Yoshichan and Noriko were placed in beds side by side at one end of the tuberculosis ward, and Micheko's duties were transferred to that floor so she might be near them. It was not easy for Micheko, knowing that her friends would soon be gone, but still it brought joy to them all for those few days, and Sensei was with them.

Noriko was taken Home first. The last night Sensei was with her, Noriko turned to her and said, a little smile on her lips:

"Remember, Sensei, when we wanted to send a present to the Crown Prince?"

Sensei smiled and nodded.

"We Japanese always want to send a present or to take one when we make a visit. What present shall I take Him?"

Sensei squeezed her hand. "You will not need to take a present," she said. "I am sending you. Tell the Lord Jesus that I am coming one day, but in the meantime I send you, and you are very precious."

Noriko slipped away that night. Yoshichan lingered for several weeks, and then she went to the comforting arms of the Lord Jesus she had loved ever since Sensei had told her about Him. Micheko and Sensei, tears in their eyes, thanked Him for taking both Yoshichan and Noriko Home where they would suffer no more heartache and trouble.

After the two girls were gone, Sensei redoubled her efforts to locate the others. It was an enormously difficult task. Bombings and wartime destruction had scattered the girls all over Japan, but one lead led to another, and in time Sensei found each girl who had been placed for adoption back in 1940. Many had suffered greatly during the war. Many had lost their homes and loved ones. But none had lost her faith in God. And as Sensei located each one, her heart lightened a little. Each reunion was joyous; a token of the covenant care of God.

13

Ochanomizu Student Center

Sensei now turned her attention to other matters. Since her return to Japan, she had not visited what had once been Sunrise Home, and now she determined to do so. She had not bothered to check on the property, and she traveled to Akashi believing that the Kobe Orphanage was housed in the Home, and hoping in her heart that it would not be too much different from the days when she had known it.

To her surprise, she found that the Orphanage had only remained in the Home for a few months. Then the government had requisitioned it for wounded soldiers, and when the war ended the Home had been turned over to teachers as a rest home. The children's laughter, the whole feeling of the Home which she had known and loved was gone, and Sensei returned to Kyoto with a heavy heart. She had tried to recapture something of another day, but it eluded her.

"The truth is," Sensei chided herself, "you had clung in your heart to the idea that you would return there and start your work over, and everything would be the same. But the Lord has other work in mind for you, and you let Him lead you!"

It was not clear to her in what direction He might be leading. MacArthur, supported by women's organizations in Japan, had smashed the powerful network which supported licensed brothels; and the old system of selling children into prostitution had largely vanished, so there was little need to reorganize Sunrise Home. She had never, of course, collected any rental on the property, so, without much hope of success, she instituted proceedings to try to reclaim it. Money from the sale of the Home could at least go into mission funds. However, the title was so beclouded, and the "scrap-of-paper" agreement Sensei had drawn up so inadequate, that her claims were never satisfied.

Sensei spent many hours asking God to show her what steps He wished her to take next, and one day in June, 1947, she received a visitor from Tokyo—a slim young lieutenant in the United States Infantry who had remained in Japan as a civilian employee of the War Department.

His name was Charles Hummel. He had been active in the Inter-Varsity Christian Fellowship while a student at Yale, and in Tokyo he had taught Bible classes at Tokyo University. Interest had been very great, and many of the students had accepted Christ.

But now he planned to return home, and he wanted Sensei to

take over his classes. Sensei had no wish at all to live in Tokyo. Conditions were extremely difficult there, and she was not sure that she wanted to work with college students. In her heart she really longed to return to some kind of work with children.

She wrestled over the problem. She talked with Dr. Saiki and even wrote to her old friend Adelaide. But they only told her what she knew they would: That the decision lay between her and the Lord.

Finally Sensei decided that the University work must be what the Lord had in mind for her. She accepted the request.

"I'm getting older," she thought, as she packed her few possessions to move once again. And she thought that again when she said good-by to Dr. Saiki and Micheko and other friends in Kyoto.

But when she reached Tokyo, though she was sixty years old now, she entered into the work with her customary energy. She soon discovered that conditions in Tokyo had not been exaggerated. Hummel had said he would find her a place to stay. He greeted her with an air of triumph—and an air mattress.

Dutifully Sensei went with him as he led the way to the Christian and Missionary Alliance Home, and there she found that her "quarters" would be the size of the air mattress—in a room already occupied by seven other women. To complete the picture, there was not enough room for her to sleep on the mattress. The problem was solved by putting it crosswise in the middle of the floor and all eight of the occupants using it as a pillow while they slept on the tatami mats!

"Oh, that floor," Sensei groaned. "After ten days I decided that my old bones wouldn't take it. I got up one night and went out on the steps—not steps like you know!" she adds. "Just slats of wood for steps and very steep. I sat down on the top step and I asked the Lord if He really wanted me in student work. 'Lord,' I said, 'if You do, You'll have to find me a room of my own in Tokyo!"

At breakfast the next morning her roommates teased her a little about preferring to sit on the steps to sleeping with her head on the "pillow" along with them.

"I was speaking to the Lord," Sensei told them firmly. "He's going to find me a room for myself."

The girls laughed, but Sensei was too old in the faith to be disturbed. "You'll see!" she told them.

That Sunday Sensei went to Friends Meeting. After the service, a charming Quaker lady came up to her.

"If thee wants a room," she said, "I think I can tell thee where thee can get one."

Sensei all but shouted her joy to the Lord. The room the Quaker lady had for her was in the home of one of the teachers at Friends Girls' School, and ten minutes after Sensei had the address, she was knocking on the door.

She was cordially greeted and shown to the second floor room. It was small but exceedingly pleasant. One window looked out on a tree-filled valley, and the sight made Sensei's heart soar.

"You may move in as soon as you like," the owner told her.

"I'll be back this afternoon!" Sensei promised.

She was a bit late getting back to the Alliance Home, and the rest were already at dinner when she slipped into her place.

"Did you miss your way?" one of the girls asked her.

Sensei beamed at her. "Oh, no!" she said. "I just took the time to go to see my new room!"

The girls looked at her in awe. "But you just prayed last night!" one of them exclaimed.

"When you have faith as a mustard seed . . . ," Sensei reminded them. And many a girl left the table that day to think more seriously about what she believed.

Sensei moved into her new room and began her classes at the University. Conditions were more than difficult. Thousands of commuting students, all eager to get a university education, jammed every available inch of space. Electricity was rationed. Charcoal was difficult to find. There was no place to study, let alone meditate or hold adequate prayer meetings, and Sensei walked the streets of the city, praying for guidance so that she could do better work.

"If I could just find one vacant room!" she thought. But that seemed impossible.

Then one day she was walking along the street near the University, her mind taken up with the devastation of war which was so starkly evident. Rubble from the bombings cluttered vacant lots. One could see burned-out houses where squatters lived perilously. Others built shacks of corrugated iron, old cartons, or whatever was available. Only the main building of Meiji University seemed to have escaped the bombs.

Suddenly she noticed a three-story stucco building just across from the University. It did not look very promising, but she walked up the staircase, poking around to find someone who might help her. She located a cell-like little office occupied by a thin-faced Japanese.

"Would it be possible for me to rent a room in this building for an hour or two a week?" she asked, knowing that she could not possibly hope for more. All rooms were rented on an hourly basis.

He shook his head. "No," he said bluntly.

Sensei tried to argue with him, but he merely shrugged. As

she was turning to leave, another Japanese who had heard the conversation, hurried up.

"I am just giving up my room," he said. "I have the use of it from three thirty to four thirty every Saturday afternoon. Would that be of help to you?"

Sensei assured him that it would be, and the stranger turned to the manager, urging him to let Sensei have the room. He gave in grumpily. Sensei gave him a month's rent in advance, and he gave her a receipt.

"Fifty minutes teaching only," he said. "Ten minutes needed to let your class go in and out."

Sensei assured him that she would abide by the rules. The Japanese who had been so helpful asked her: "What are you teaching?"

"Bible study," Sensei beamed. "I introduce my students to my great Friend, the Lord Jesus Christ."

There was a moment of stunned silence. Then the manager began to shout. The previous tenant scuttled away rapidly.

"You can only have that room for a month!" the manager shouted at Sensei. "If I'd known what you teach, I wouldn't have let you have it for an hour!"

Sensei made a quick exit. A policeman was standing at the corner, and curious as always, Sensei stopped and asked him who owned the three-story building just up the street.

"I rented a room there," she said, "and when they found out what I teach, they raised a great rumpus!"

"What *do* you teach?" the policeman asked.

"Bible study," Sensei told him.

The policeman laughed. "Madam," he said. "I should think that they must have made quite a stir. That building, Madam, is the headquarters of the Communist Party!"

Communist Party headquarters or no, Sensei made very good use of her hour-a-week rental. Students flocked to the room, and it did Sensei's heart secret good to know how disgruntled it must make the owners to see how popular her Bible classes were.

Her work at the University got off to a slow start—there was a good deal of hostility, but Sensei reminded herself that the Lord's work flourished in a hostile climate, and indeed it did. Very soon she had a larger group of very loyal supporters.

But as the membership grew, it became very evident to Sensei that she must establish a real student center. She shrank from the thought of looking for property, but she set about the task, enlisting the services of several banks and trusts. At the end of the month she lost her Red Headquarters room. There was no place else to be had. She had to confine her work to her University classes.

About this time the local manager of the British Overseas Airways Corporation gave Sensei two Quonset huts which had served as temporary offices. She had them stored away, thinking that some day she might find a piece of land on which to erect them, and perhaps they would serve as her longed-for student union.

One day a missionary of the Evangelical Alliance Mission called her and asked if she had any idea where he might find some building material. Sensei told him that she did not have, but afterwards her conscience bothered her.

"I'm a regular dog in the manager!" she told herself. "That man could probably use those huts, and here I am storing them away in the hopes I can use them for myself. Please forgive me, Lord, though I don't deserve it!"

She promptly called the official of the Alliance and told him he could have the huts. He was overwhelmed with gratitude and told her then how desperately he had needed them.

"I'll pray that you find a house," he told her.

"And I will, too," the old lady said.

On the following Saturday afternoon as Sensei was leaving a prayer meeting, a young girl came up to her.

"Excuse me," she said, "but my father is the president of the Chuo Trust Company. He is sorry that he couldn't locate property where you could erect your Quonset huts, but he asked me to tell you about a house near here. He says you should go to see it. It is listed as sold, but my father does not think the final papers have been signed. He says to tell you that you should offer six million four hundred and eighty thousand yen."*

Sensei planted herself firmly on the sidewalk in front of the girl. She blinked nearsightedly at her through her thick spectacles.

"And where is this house?" she asked.

"Next to the building where you were holding your meetings," the girl said, and gave her the address.

"Thank you," Sensei said, bobbing a bow. "Thank you very much, dear."

She stumped off, a squat, gallant, fiercely independent old lady, wondering why, if there were such a house, the broker himself had not called.

"Don't you be arguing with the Lord," she told herself as she marched along. "He knows better than you do!"

Without a moment's hesitation she tramped up the stairs of the Red headquarters, gave a nod to the manager who shouted at her that she no longer was a tenant.

"I know that!" she said, giving him a straight look. "But

* $18,000.

there's nothing in your building laws that says I can't go up to the roof to have a look about, is there?"

Before the apoplectic manager could regain his wits, Sensei had marched on to the roof. She peered over the edge of it, looking down at the property she had been told might be for sale. It was a fine property. There was a two-story building, sheltered by trees, and a low one-story Japanese house. She saw an entrance on the main street, which pleased her, and all in all, her roof-side view told her that the property would be admirable.

Sensei went back down the stairs, nodded to the still-sputtering manager, and went out the front door. There was something very magnificent about this old gray-haired lady as she approached the gated entrance of the next-door property. A tradesman was knocking at the gate, but Sensei with a nod went past him. She sounded the knocker on the front door of the building.

A maid answered.

"May I see the owner of the house?" Sensei asked her.

The little maid went away and soon came back to usher Sensei inside. A handsome elderly woman came to greet her, polite inquiry in her eyes. Sensei wasted no time.

"Is it true," she asked, "that you wish to sell this property?"

The woman looked a little startled by so direct an approach, but she inclined her head slightly. "It is true," she said. And added with a small reprimand to Sensei for her bluntness: "My name is Asada San."

Sensei bowed. "I am Smith Sensei," she said. "And I am in search of a place to carry out the work of my Friend, who is the Savior."

There was a hint of curiosity in the woman's eyes, but she

spoke in the same even polite tones. "I am very sorry, Smith Sensei. But bids have already been offered on this house, and the two top bids were equal. We have asked the bidders to resubmit."

Sensei drew in a long breath. "I am sorry, too," she said. "I had hoped I might buy it."

The woman, far too well bred to appear to survey her visitor openly, nevertheless did study her. "Why do you want the house?" she asked.

Sensei explained, and as she talked her very words seemed to reflect that inspiration which had so dominated her whole life.

"I was told to offer six million four hundred and eighty thousand yen," Sensei finished. And then a pure Irish smile lighted her face. "To tell you the truth," she confessed, "I do not have that much money—I don't even have six thousand yen. But if you trust me, you will never be sorry. He has never failed me, and I know He won't this time!"

Asada San did not answer directly. Instead she said: "You're the lady who used to conduct meetings from the third floor next door."

Sensei nodded. "That I am," she said. "And rousing meetings they were, too! That's why I want to find better quarters now that my Red landlords have thrown me out!"

A smile touched the woman's lips. "I will tell you something," she said. "I used to hear you—every word. I was caught first just by the chance hearing of a few words, but after that I found if I sat on my upper veranda, I could hear all you said."

Sensei beamed at her. "Now that's wonderful!" she said. "I'm glad you could hear! And I hope you were interested."

The woman nodded, but she did not answer directly. "Those

were University boys there, weren't they?" she asked. Sensei said that they were. The woman went on: "I had two sons. They were University students, too—like those boys. But they were killed in the war. And my husband, too."

"Ah, now I am sorry!" Sensei said honestly. "I'm sure they were good lads! I wish they could have been with us up there in our small room."

They talked a few moments more, but Asada San made no direct mention of the property. "I am sorry you came too late," she told Sensei as she ushered her out.

Sensei replied: "Asada San, my God is never too late. He's always on time . . . if you consider my offer, that will be wonderful, but if this property is not for us, we don't want it."

"Well," Sensei thought as she trudged towards home. "It was a pleasant chat, anyway."

She was not feeling well the next day, and since she had no classes, she determined to stay at home and rest for a change. She stretched out on her bed, looking forward to what she called a "selfish day."

She had not been there more than an hour when her landlady called her and told here there had been a message. She was to go to the home of Asada San at once. The landlady gave her the address, but Sensei did not need it.

Putting on her good serviceable walking suit and her stout boots, she set out at once. She no more thought of hailing a cab than she had that day so long ago when she and Adelaide set out for the Royal Garden Party. Gray-haired Sensei still traveled on shanks' mare.

Back at Asada San's home she was ushered into a small, beautifully appointed sitting room. Her hostess apologized for calling her back, and then, leaning towards her, asked her directly: "How do you worship your God?"

For a moment Sensei was taken aback. Then she said: "Well, we sit quietly, as we are here. We do not have to be formal. We close our eyes and praise Him for all He is to us—for being our wonderful God."

"You do not need a shrine?" Asada San asked.

Sensei shook her head. "Our God is always with us," she said. "We need no shrine."

"You need nothing at all?" the woman persisted.

Sensei looked at her. "We need Christian love to gather together on the Lord's Day and worship Him, but we need no shrine," Sensei said.

Asada San sat deep in thought. Then she rose abruptly. Beckoning to Sensei, she said: "Please follow me."

Sensei obeyed. Asada San led Sensei into her own private apartment. Sensei had seldom seen anything so delicately beautiful. Everything seemed to have been planned to make a symphony of color and line.

Asada San pushed back the shoji at one end of the apartment. A small room was revealed with a window in the back, shaped like a lotus flower. In front of it was a long lacquer shelf on which rested a huge bowl of white chrysanthemums, and beside it were photographs of her husband and two sons.

Mrs. Asada San said: "I come here every day. I have said hundreds of prayers here."

She stepped forward and touched a black and gold lacquered cabinet inlaid with mother of pearl. "This is my shrine," she said. "But though I pray here, my prayers are not answered."

With a sudden move she opened the doors of the cabinet. Three jars stood there. She pointed to them.

"This is all I have," she said. "These are my loved ones."

Sensei said nothing, for in truth so many thoughts were teeming in her mind that she did not know what to say. She felt the sorrow and emptiness Asada San lived with, and she longed to pour out words of Christ's comfort, but she could not quite find the one with which to begin.

Asada San closed the cabinet. "I will have it taken out," she said. "I know you will not want it."

Sensei gaped at her. "But you said—," she stammered. "I mean—you told me you already had two bidders—."

"So I have," the woman said. "They both bid seven million two hundred thousand yen. They were to come today to outbid each other, the property to go to whoever bid higher."

"But—!" Sensei sputtered.

"Do you not want the property?" Asada San asked.

"Of course!" Sensei cried. "But I only bid six million four hundred and eighty thousand yen, and you know I told you I didn't have a bit of that!"

"But we will trust your God," Asada San smiled. "Isn't that right?"

"Yes," Sensei said, joy surging through her.

"The property is yours," Asada San said.

Sensei, who was very seldom at a loss for words, very nearly was now. She thanked Asada San as best as she could and made her departure, never even thinking of such things as signed agreements. In due time a messenger brought her a full set of legal documents for her signature, and Sensei found that she had been given the entire plot on which the building stood—the two-story house, and an adjoining one-story building, plus a little concrete storehouse.

"Lord," Sensei said, as she dropped to her knees, "I do thank

Thee for what You are doing." She stayed silent a moment trying to gather her sixty-plus years together for what lay ahead. Suddenly her back stiffened, and the old fire was in her. "Don't you let me fall short on any payment now, Lord!" she said . . . "even if I'm a church mouse with big, grand ideas!"

Sensei found her way through the legal end of the matter as best she could. Such details always fussed her, and she did not half understand them. But the gist of it was that in spite of a good deal of muttering and concern from her superiors, the JEB would hold title to this land she had purchased—on promises, as they said, and that title would be in trust for the IVCF. A good deal of controversy ensued, and finally Sensei insisted that a committee of nationals and missionaries should operate and control the proposed student center. When it was all finally settled, Sensei breathed a sigh of relief.

In the spring of 1950 Sensei moved into her new quarters. She hadn't a piece of furniture, and she hadn't thought of how to get any.

"What are you going to do?" Mrs. Oliver, an American friend, whose husband was a civilian engineer working in Tokyo, asked her.

"I haven't thought about it," Sensei said. "If I had a lot of furniture now, I'd just be facing a bigger moving chore. I'll just leave it in His hands."

The woman shook her head. Sometimes, she thought, you really wanted to shake Sensei! In some ways, she was so impractical.

Sensei, sublimely oblivious to such thoughts, moved what few things she had collected for her one room into the grand house. They looked a little lost, she admitted—one worn easy chair, one folding chair and her bed.

Sensei arranged them as comfortably as possible and proceeded to invite everyone who had helped her move to tea. It was all very gay. People sat on the floor good naturedly, and Sensei, a little flustered with excitement and happiness, bustled about, offering cakes and making sure that everyone's tea was hot.

Midway in the party, Mrs. Oliver, her American friend appeared in the doorway.

"Could you have the main gates opened?" she asked.

"Of course!" Sensei cried. "Have you come by car? I never thought of anyone coming by car! How splendid."

She clapped her hands and told the houseboy to open the gates at once as they had a guest who wished to pull her car in. Mrs. Oliver merely smiled and said nothing. But a few minutes later men began carrying handsome bamboo furniture into the room. There were chairs and tables and a sofa and a coffee table. Sensei was dumbfounded.

"But this is your furniture!" she cried. "This is from your own house!"

Mrs. Oliver still merely smiled. And the men, making other trips, carried in a complete dining room set.

"But how will you manage?" Sensei cried.

"Very well," Mrs. Oliver said. "We can get Occupation furniture, and it's quite good enough for us."

"But I can't take your beautiful furniture and leave you with such things!" Sensei cried, almost in tears.

"Ah, Sensei!" Mrs. Oliver said, smiling fondly at her. "It's not you who is taking. We're giving these things—giving them to the Lord's work."

Sensei was very nearly overcome. Her quick Irish wit seemed to desert her, and she turned helplessly from one guest to another as they set about arranging the furniture.

"Ah, to think I'd have such good friends!" Sensei choked when at last the guests were taking their leave.

That night Sensei went to bed tired but happy. It hardly seemed possible. She was really in the new student center. Oh, it wasn't ready yet, but it would be—it would be. And then what grand meetings there'd be and what rejoicing.

"And places for those lads to study, too, Lord," she said as she fell into tired sleep. "Now they need a little quiet, and good books. We'll see they have them, yes, Lord?"

Sensei threw all of her efforts into the new student union. She worked day and night, and those who knew her marveled at the strength and energy of the aging Irishwoman. The friendly rooms were soon crowded with eager students, in their search. Sensei was never too tired to sit and talk about Christ, never too tired to hear a personal problem, never too tired to bring someone to Christ. And many came. The student center seemed to be a very part of God's work in a modern world, and Sensei who had begun her dedication so many years before, found this exhilarating.

"They need You more now than they ever did, Lord," she said. "And they're searching for You. And it is wonderful to be a part of their finding You."

14

Last Rites for Mr. Miki

A year went by almost before Sensei knew it, and she woke one morning suddenly feeling very tired.

"I need a rest," she said to herself.

Suddenly she thought of Karuizawa where in the days of JEB work she had always found such refreshment of spirit.

"I'm going there!" she said.

She never stopped to think how many years it had been since the days of Karuizawa. Sensei was a marvelous combination of practicality and total impracticality.

She packed her bags, turned over her classes to assistants, and set off for the rest home, never doubting for a moment that it would be exactly as she remembered it. Indeed, she probably thought that she would meet Jim and Clara Cuthbertson and Adelaide, perhaps even Miss Penrod. Perhaps not in the flesh, but in spirit at least.

She was full of anticipation as she got off the train, and she never bothered to ask anyone if the rest home were actually available to anyone these days. Grasping her bag, she trudged up the hill, her hat a little crooked on her iron-gray hair, her steps a good deal slower than they had been that day when they had climbed to see the volcano. It was a *long* time ago.

She reached the retreat. But everything was changed. There was no busy chatter of missionaries filling the air, no quick coming and going through the always-open and welcoming door. The rest home looked older. A fence had been put up around it, and a few straggly flowers grew in the front yard. Some children were playing there, and they stopped in their play and stared at her curiously as, very tired, she sat her bag down and looked at the house.

She smiled at them a little uncertainly. "Are there rooms for let?" she asked.

They stared at her silently, not answering. She repeated her question. Suddenly a woman appeared at the doorway, and Sensei asked her the same question, adding: "I used to come here often when I was younger. This was our rest home, you know."

"No rooms," the woman said. "Our house now."

Then Sensei realized that the lovely old rest home was now private property. She started to turn away, but then the old spirit flared in her again. "How did you come to live here?" she asked pleasantly.

The woman shrugged. "Government," she said.

But that property still belongs to the JEB, Sensei thought. And that means it belongs to the Lord, for His purpose.

A mental note was filed away in her head, but at the moment she only asked if she might have a drink of water, and after a good deal of haggling about who should take it to her, one of the children brought her a cupful. She thanked him but he merely turned away, and the noisy play in the yard resumed; the woman went into the house.

Sensei felt nostalgic and very old. The bag in her hand was suddenly too heavy, and she knew she must have some refreshment of spirit before she started her journey home. Instinctively she turned toward the stream where the missionaries had so often gone to find places of meditation. It seemed to be the only real link with the past. She followed it a ways, and found a lovely shaded place to sit. The air was fresh and cool. The water in the small stream seemed to sparkle and dance, and Sensei dipped her old hands into it. It was cold and clear, and she felt its revitalizing freshness lift her.

"Lord," she whispered. . . . "Thou art the same, and thy years shall not fail."

She stayed by the stream until she was rested and refreshed, and as she went back to take the train to Tokyo, her step was light as a young girl's.

Back in Tokyo she was plunged almost immediately into the necessity of finding larger quarters for the student Christian center. As she sat thinking about it she was reminded of the words Amy Carmichael had written to her many years before: . . . "*don't build too small . . . at times I have been led into trying to make economies only to find that in the long run they were costly. . . .*"

"Well," Sensei said, sitting up, back straight. "I'm going to do *this* right! It may be the last chance I have to do a really grand job for the Lord."

She didn't know exactly what the "grand job" would be, but her first thought was to get the two houses on the main street moved back to the rear of the property so that a fine modern building could be erected where they now were.

She consulted architects and engineers, and they all told her, firmly but politely, that it was impossible. The buildings she wanted moved were of concrete. The only thing to do if she wanted to build on the front of the property, they told her, was to put a bulldozer through the old buildings.

Sensei's innate sense of thrift, shrank from the very thought of tearing down perfectly good buildings. She had met every payment, though she had started with almost nothing. Asada San, though she did not see her, always sent polite little notes in acknowledgement of each payment. And Sensei felt that, the property having come to her as it did, she would not readily relinquish.

"I'm not going to destroy those buildings!" she said to herself. But what was she to do?

She sought counsel from the Scriptures, and one line caught her eye: "The house was moved at the posts of the doors."

Now what does that mean? Sensei thought. She was sure it meant something. The next day she called in a house mover named Gusti and asked him about moving the house. As usual, he said it could not be done.

"Will you go downstairs and look at the foundations?" she asked.

Reluctantly, the man did. When he came up, he said:

"Well, perhaps it can be done. We can cut it off at the foundations and have new foundations laid further back. But it will be expensive. And you take the responsibility."

Sensei made no commitment. She called in another house mover and asked him the same thing. After due consideration, he told her the same thing Gusti had and quoted nearly the same price.

"Do you know Gusti?" she asked.

"I certainly ought to!" the man said.

"Are you friends?" Sensei asked.

The man glared at her. "We're rivals," he said.

Sensei surveyed him with a quizzical air. Suddenly she said. "Now I tell you what is going to happen. You and Gusti are going to move this house together. I'm going to give you a contract. And I will take full responsibility for whatever happens."

The man stared at her as though she had gone mad, but Sensei merely beamed at him with total assurance. And in the end, it was the two rivals who moved the house. Not a crack developed. Not a single floor sagged.

Now Sensei started her plans for the new building. It must include an auditorium, classrooms, offices, and a library. It must be a building which would attract the thousands of students who passed the site each day. This was a vision as great as that which she had known when she knew she must start Sunrise Home, for into her new building hundreds of students would come. They would learn about Christ's word. They would come to Him and accept Him. And from this building she envisioned, they would go out into the land and bear a witness for Him.

"Oh, Lord! . . . except the Lord build the house they labor in vain who build it—let it be worthy of Thy Name."

Sensei ran into a great deal of opposition. A good many people thought she was too high-handed, and some of her board members felt that she did not consult them often enough. Sensei was not used to consulting anyone. She was used to getting things done.

And this she did. Including the student center, which she was convinced was the best way to bring the greatest number of students to hear the Message.

She wanted a three story building, but the governing board, which Sensei was already calling her "restraining board," conservatively decided that two was enough. Sensei did not argue. But she had a concrete stairway built, leading to a nonexistent third story, and she had the construction men put the steel reinforcement rods high enough for at least one more story.

"I didn't go against the Board," she said, "but I made sure the Lord's work could be completed, right and proper!"

In March, 1951, the first two stories were ready for use. Sensei could scarcely wait for the opening evangelistic services to be held.

There were a good many critics. The building had cost too much, they said. It was folly to have rooms where students could meet informally—they would only misuse them. The whole thing was a bad investment.

Sensei sat back in her chair. She looked smaller now somehow. All the labors, all the work, all the years had made her body smaller. But the spirit which blazed from her eyes was stronger than ever. She was an indomitable old lady as she sat there facing her critics before the dedication.

"The Lord showed the way!" she said, her voice ringing with conviction. "And I followed that way! We want to lead students to Christ, and in this student center that is what we will do!"

The opening day came. The critics who had predicted stay-away crowds were engulfed by the students who thronged in. The whole new student center seemed alive with their zeal, and on that very night of the opening there many who came to Christ.

But in later years, Sensei's critics had to face not only the truth that she had been right about the student center being a place to lead young people to Christ, but the very practical fact that her $18,000 investment was financially far more than sound. By 1964 the student center property value, by conservative estimates, was worth over $1,000,000!

Sensei, who had only a few yen in her pocket when she bought the Asada home, had made good on her promise to meet every payment, had acquired property which had appreciated by more than 1,000 per cent in a short fourteen years.

But if anyone ever asked her about it, she would only look a little astounded and say with her whole heart: "But 'what shall it profit a man if he gain the whole world?' It is the *students* who have come to know Jesus Christ as personal Savior and Friend. . . . I call that real grand!"

Sensei had worked harder than she knew in getting the student center opening and running, and she suddenly found herself very tired. She was desperately in need of a rest, but she had no funds at all—they had all been put into the building.

Suddenly without any warning, she received a call from Lady Sekiya, wife of the controller of the Imperial Household and, like her husband, a Quaker convert.

Lady Sekiya told Sensei that, as a lady in waiting, she had been appointed to take charge of the children of the Imperial Household, and that they would be staying at a resort for six weeks.

"We should like you to accompany us," Lady Sekiya said.

Sensei felt baffled. "As your guest?" she asked.

"We should be honored," Lady Sekiya said in her lovely low voice. "And perhaps you would also conduct morning worship for the little children. We would most gladly supply you with a small house of your own for the entire summer. You would not need to worry about the children at other times," she added. "There will be other ladies in waiting and servants to care for them."

Mercy me! Sensei thought to herself. *Now I've really come full circle!*

But, she thought, I was wishing for a bit of rest at some nice cool place, and now the Lord has provided this opportunity. If there's a bit of work connected with it, it's probably to keep me from getting too soft!

She accepted the invitation, and in a few weeks, she found herself settled at a beautiful resort, surrounded with every luxury. The cottage she occupied was gracious and charming. A servant was appointed to attend her every need. For Sensei, who had handled so many babies, her duties were not difficult.

She was anxious to see that the children under her care got the best instruction she could give, and she decided on a theme for the summer teaching: "What the Lord Jesus Christ said about Himself."

She started with the expression, "I am meek and lowly in heart." The children listened enthralled as she told what this meant and gave them stories which showed how the life of Jesus bore out the sentence.

Next she talked to them about the words: "I am the bread of life; I am the water of life; I am the light of the world."

The children enjoyed the classes and the devotional periods, and like children everywhere, they adored Sensei. She made no distinction between the royal children and the children of palace officials and lords and ladies in waiting. This was in keeping with the royal family's wish to have a normal atmosphere for the children to grow up in, and Sensei had been well aware of it before she went to the resort. Indeed, on one occasion when she had been a guest in the Sekiya home, she was told in advance to take no notice of the "maid" who dropped to her knees, shoved back the sliding door and bowed low with her eyes to the ground. Later she found out that the "maid" was one of the royal children who was serving as a domestic as part of her training. You may be sure that practical Sensei believed in such training.

One of the pleasant aspects of the summer for Sensei was the companionship of Elizabeth Vining, a Philadelphia Quaker, and tutor to Crown Prince Akihito. The two had tea together and went on occasional picnics, and Sensei found these times deeply rewarding.

But delightful as the summer was, Sensei could hardly wait to get back to her work. "I'm like an old war horse," she thought. "Always eager to be in harness."

She was destined, however, to have another rest from her work much sooner than she had counted on—this one enforced. When the houses had been moved to the back of the student union property, alterations had been made in a staircase, and one of the railings had not been properly secured. One day Sensei was leaning against it. It gave way, and she fell.

She was rushed to St. Luke's Hospital, where it was discovered she had broken her shoulder. It was necessary to encase her in a cast from neck to waist. For once Sensei actually had to stop work entirely.

The stream of visitors who came to see her, and the cards and flowers she received were a testimony to how widely she was loved and respected. She had friends among the high and the lowly. The Emperor's youngest brother, Prince Mekasa, who called himself "one of Sensei's lost sheep" because through her he had found Christ, and his lovely Princess and their children were as fond of Sensei as the shopkeeper on the corner. Missionaries, her old Sunrise girls, students, GI's, generals, lords and ladies in waiting, teachers and businessmen—people from all walks of life came to see her while she was hospitalized, and Sensei's old heart was touched.

"To think that the Lord could have been so good to me . . . in His service 'the lines have fallen onto me in pleasant places.' " Finally recovered, she went back to her work with a happy heart.

She had not been back in her old quarters long before she had a visitor. She did not recognize him at first. The man before her was thin and ill looking. Suddenly she knew.

"Mr. Miki!" she cried, taking his hands. "Oh, come in! Come in!"

She led him into her sitting room and ordered tea. Memories of the days in Akashi flooded through her, and she was more touched than she could find words to express at seeing her old friend.

She and the former president of the Osaka Stock Exchange sat for a long time talking. Mr. Miki lived very simply now in a small village some miles distant. His wife had died, and three of his sons had been killed in the war. Only Yoshiko, who was married, was left of the children Sensei had known and loved so well.

"I remarried," Mr. Miki told her, "and I have a young son. We have little of worldly goods, but we have the Lord Jesus Christ. Often we have neighbors into our home to talk of Him. Many around us have come to Christ, too."

Mr. Miki had brought Sensei a bag of potatoes he had grown himself—true to Japanese custom he would not pay a visit without bringing some gift. Sensei insisted that he stay to supper with her, and they talked over old times until he had to leave.

She was worried about him—he didn't look well. And when he came some weeks later to see her again, bringing this time a bag of clams he had dug along the shore for her, Sensei saw that he had failed even more.

"Dear friend," she said, "isn't there something I can do?"

He smiled. "You are doing much," he said. "Seeing you and talking with you is reviving to my spirit. Will you pray with me, Sensei?"

They knelt and prayed together, and then the former broker said he must go. Sensei urged him to stay at least for dinner. But he shook his head.

"I have not time, Sensei," he said, and there was a gentle note in his voice.

She let him go, but she could not get him out of her mind. Sleep would not come to her that night. She kept hearing Mr. Miki's last words.

A few days later Sensei received a telegram from his widow, stating that Mr. Miki had died.

She decided that she would drop everything to go to the funeral. She wanted to pay her last respects to this Christian warrior who had borne so much because of his testimony for Christ.

The feeling inside of her was too strong to ignore. "I must go to Mr. Miki," she said to her maid. "I must go at once."

She checked trains, but there was none until late in the day, and Sensei could not wait. She remembered a missionary colleague, John Schwab, who had a station wagon, and she called him and asked him if he could drive her to the seaside village.

"Of course," he said. "I'll be there at once."

Sensei took her Bible and a copy of the Gospel of John. At

the last moment, for a reason she herself could not explain, she decided to take her portable phonograph and two records: "Face to Face with Christ, My Savior," and "Safe in the Arms of Jesus."

They made good time on the highway and reached the village in the late afternoon. It took them a little time to find the Miki home, and when they got there, they found a crowd of people in the front yard. Men were driving the last nails into a plain wooden coffin they had just made.

Sensei hurried into the cottage. There, the widow and her son were kneeling beside Mr. Miki's coffin, was the body of Mr. Miki lying on the tatami, his Bible, *Daily Light,* and a hymn book at his side. For a moment Sensei could not move, and then she, too, knelt in prayer.

When she rose, the widow came to her. "You are Sensei," she said.

Sensei nodded, her heart too full for words.

"My husband said you would come," Mrs. Miki said. "It was his wish that you conduct his funeral."

Sensei had never conducted a funeral, but she knew now why God had put the urgency of this visit in her heart. She knew why she had brought the records and the Gospel.

Solemnly the body of Mr. Miki was placed in the coffin, and his Bible put in his hands. The group gathered around the coffin, and Sensei, her old voice quavering, started a hymn. John Schwab's strong voice joined hers.

Sensei spoke then of Mr. Miki, of his life and of his faith. "He became a Christian at great cost," she said. "He lost many possessions. Yet he found great riches in the Lord Jesus, Who has now received him into His presence."

Softly, John played one of the hymns Sensei had brought. He

read the twenty-third Psalm and then the little assemblage knelt in prayer. The last hymn was played.

Solemnly, the coffin was lifted to the back of the station wagon, and the humble procession of mourners escorted it to the crematory.

Back at the small cottage, the widow came to Sensei. "God undertakes for our every need," she said softly, "and He has shown us again today how true that is. May I show you something?"

"Of course," Sensei said.

Mrs. Miki took a small list from a near-by shelf. "This list my husband wrote," she said. "It is what he wished for his funeral."

She handed the list to Sensei, who read: "I should like Sensei to conduct my funeral. I wish two hymns played: 'Face to Face with Christ, my Savior,' and 'Safe in the Arms of Jesus,' and I should like the twenty-third Psalm read."

She thought of the faithfulness of God. Had not Christ said, "Whatsoever ye shall ask in my name, I will do it."

Silently Sensei handed the list back. Her eyes were misty; her heart most humble.

15

Miracles at Sugamo

Was it chance that brought Sensei to another phase of her work at an age when most people are enjoying retirement?

Noshi San, one of Sensei's former little Sunbeams, had married a widower with four children and lived in the country town of Kashiwa, a few miles from Tokyo. There was no church, no Christian witness of any kind, in the little town, and Noshi San started a Sunday school in her own home. Many of the children of the community attended, and as usually happened, the children brought their mothers. Now Noshi San wrote to Sensei, asking her if she would come and speak to the women.

Sensei accepted the invitation, and a week later made the trip to Kashiwa. The service was well-attended, and the women drank in every word Sensei said.

After the meeting was over, one of the women came up to Sensei and introduced herself.

"I am the wife of Nishizawa San," she said.

Sensei felt a moment of shock. She knew, as did everyone else in Japan, that Nishizawa San was one of the military leaders convicted of war crimes and held in Sugamo Prison, condemned to death.

"I know the Savior myself," Mrs. Nishizawa said. "But I am deeply concerned about my husband. I want very much for him to become a Christian before he dies."

Sensei was deeply touched, and she promised to pray for Nishizawa San.

His wife wanted something more. "Can't you go to see him?" she begged.

Sensei did not see how it could be managed. But Mrs. Nishizawa pleaded with her. "I am allowed to visit my husband a half an hour each month," she said. "On my last trip I took him the Gospel of John, but he was not interested. If you could go, I know you could reach him. I will give up my visiting privilege for you."

Sensei could not refuse. She knew it would not be easy to get permission. The men at Sugamo had been convicted by the International War Crimes Tribunal, and they were held under tight security. But difficulties had never stopped Sensei yet, and she was not about to let them now.

When she returned to Tokyo, she went directly to the legal section of general headquarters and made a formal request to visit Nishizawa San.

She was turned down. "No one can see the prisoner except his wife, his mother, or his lawyer," she was told brusquely.

"Now there must be some way!" Sensei said, peering like a teacher through her spectacles at the young officer. "Everything can be arranged if we have patience and our reason is good."

"And what *is* your reason?" the officer demanded.

"His wife wishes me to visit him," Sensei said. "She has even offered to give up her precious thirty minutes to me."

This seemed to affect the officer. He hesitated a moment and then went into an inner office. After some time a colonel came out and questioned Sensei, and eventually she was questioned by a third officer. They asked her to wait, and they conducted a lengthy conference. Finally she was called into the office again.

"Are you a priest?" her interrogators asked her.

"No," Sensei said, "I could hardly make that claim."

There were more deliberations, and finally the colonel spoke to her again. "Every condemned man has the privilege of one clemency interview with a priest on some religious person," he said. "No woman has ever acted in this capacity."

Sensei smiled. "I have been a 'religious person' for many years," she said. "And I am a woman."

The colonel went on to tell her how closely the prison was guarded. "We must take every precaution," he said. "Just recently one of the wives of a prisoner smeared poison on the wire mesh of the interview booth. Her husband licked it off and died."

Sensei pressed her lips firmly together and said nothing.

At last the American officer said: "We have decided that since this man is entitled to one clemency interview, we will let you see him. *Providing* this is his choice. We must ask him first if he wants to see you."

Sensei bowed her thanks and went home to wait.

Some days later she was notified that Nishizawa would see her.

She journeyed to the prison. It was a great gray stone building, its very appearance grim and foreboding. Sensei's purse was taken from her, and she was checked carefully to see that she carried no article which the prisoner might use to take his life. At last she was led through grim corridors to the interview booth. Two guards took their places at the entrance behind her. The heavy wire mesh was in front of her. Nishizawa was led into his side of the booth and sat facing her. Guards stood behind him, too.

"I have seen your wife and children," Sensei began, "and they are well. I met her at a Christian service."

Nishizawa nodded. "She told me she had been converted," he said, and the tone of his voice showed no interest. "She left me a booklet."

That would be the Gospel, of course, and it gave Sensei the opening she had been looking for. She explained that Christ had died for the sins of men and that He offered to forgive them, if they would truly repent . . . Not only that, they would become His children and live eternally with Him.

"As many as receive him," she quoted from the first chapter of John "to them gave He power to become the sons of God, even to them that believe on His name."

She went on talking, putting all her confidence in every word, and Nishizawa's interest began to grow.

"Do you mean He could forgive *my* sins?" he asked.

"Yes, surely," Sensei said.

"Do you know what they are?" he blurted. "I have committed terrible sins. You cannot imagine what they are!"

"I don't know what your sin may be," Sensei said firmly, "but I know that in the blood of Jesus Christ there is cleansing for *all* sin."

For a moment, the Japanese looked at her through the screen intently.

"What must I do to get this forgiveness?" he asked.

"Believe on the Lord Jesus Christ and thou shalt be saved," Sensei said.

She began to pray for the man's salvation, and her words reached out to him. He bowed his head, and Sensei could see that he was greatly moved. She began the words of committal to Jesus Christ as Lord and Savior, and Nishizawa repeated them after her. His hands gripped together, and he remained with head bowed and lips moving in prayer when Sensei finished. At last he looked up.

"Thank God," he whispered. "And thank you."

The soldier behind Sensei tapped her on the shoulder, telling her that her time was up.

"Just a few more minutes," Sensei said with firm authority, and the guard stepped back.

"I want to read to you," she said to Nishizawa, "from the fourteenth chapter of John." And she began: "Let not your heart be troubled. . . ." for she knew that Nishizawa was soon to die.

When she had finished, she looked into his face. "Nishizawa San," she said, "do you believe that the Lord Jesus has saved you today?"

"Yes, I do," he answered quietly.

"I want you to do something for me," Sensei said. "I want you to find some one person in the prison and tell him what the Lord has done for you. Will you do that?"

"How can I?" he said. "I am in solitary confinement."

"There is some way," Sensei said with conviction.

"At exercise time," Nishizawa said. "I will find a way then, though we are not supposed to talk. I will pass on Christ's message of salvation!"

"The Lord be with thee," Sensei said, and then bidding him good-by, she let the guards escort her out.

She went immediately to Nishizawa's wife and told her all that had happened. With tears in her eyes, Mrs. Nishizawa whispered:

"I am so glad! I have been afraid—terribly afraid—that my husband would die without salvation. Now there is no more fear, for whatever he did on earth, I know his sins are forgiven and he will be received in Heaven by our Lord!"

Sensei stayed with her a little longer, giving her comfort and reassurance. Then she went back to her own quarters, feeling that her mission had been accomplished.

Not quite a week later, Sensei received a call from general headquarters asking her to report there. When she arrived, the same colonel who had spoken to her before, asked her if she knew a man named Shibano. Sensei said that she had never heard of such a person.

"He wants to see you," the colonel said. "He, too, is in Sugamo, and he wants a clemency interview with you."

Sensei's old face lighted with joy. She knew that Nishizawa had brought a soul to Christ.

So Sensei's new work for the Lord was begun. One by one the prisoners passed the word on—their witness of what Jesus Christ had done for them, and now meant to them—and one by one they asked for clemency interviews with Sensei. She provided Testaments for all of the war criminals. and she prayed for them.

In all, fourteen of the war criminals accepted Christ through her. Thirteen of them later asked for baptism, and the rite was performed by a Baptist prison chaplain. It was a remarkable experience for Sensei, and she felt that God had indeed filled her cup to overflowing.

One morning Sensei woke with the same feeling of urgency she had felt on the day she knew she must go to Mr. Miki. This time the call was to Nishizawa San.

She hurried immediately to headquarters, asking permission. But the single interview permitted had been used. She was refused.

Sensei straightened her shoulders. There was one man in Japan who could open the prison doors for her: General MacArthur. She marched straight to his offices and requested to see him. In short order the request was granted, and she was ushered into the presence of the man who ruled all Japan. He rose and received her graciously.

Sensei told him why she had come. The general nodded and issued an order. Sensei had her permission to see Nishizawa. The General provided a staff car to take her to the prison.

In the interview room, Nishizawa was brought in to her. His face was glowing with inward joy.

"Only this morning I asked God to send you to see me!" he said.

"I know," Sensei said.

"I want to give you instructions for the care of my wife and children," he said. "And a last message for them and for my parents."

"When must you die?" Sensei asked quietly.

He shook his head. "I do not know exactly," he said. "But I know it is soon. One morning officials will enter the prisoners' dining room, and two names will be called. Mine will be one of them. We will die at midnight."

He gave Sensei the instructions he had for his family's care and his last messages to them. Then they prayed together, and Sensei noticed that this time the military policeman behind her removed his helmet and bowed his head.

As she left the prison, the guard walked with her to the green prison gates. She asked him if he was a Christian.

"My mother taught me to pray," he said, "and I used to go to Sunday school, but I haven't prayed since then." He hesitated a moment. Then he said: "You know, we've been watching you come in and out of the prison, and we've seen the changes in the men. We wondered—would you come and talk to us some time?"

Sensei agreed, and so new work started. She began a very successful series of meetings with the military police. "Step by step," she murmured to herself.

Shortly after her last visit to Nishizawa, she received a letter. She opened it and read:

Mother Smith:

I appreciate you sincerely and that you saw me again and gave me kind encouragement, sharing your busy time; and also thank you by the name of the Lord with the other brethren, hearing that the favor of baptism was realized by your unusual efforts.

I am living thankful days believing that I may receive salvation of the Holy Ghost on my last day, and entirely trusting in Him, that "for me (saved by the grace of God) to live is Christ and to die is gain."

Please give your kind direction to my family and also to the families of the following persons: (Here he listed the names and addresses of six families).

I pray your good health by the name of the Lord Jesus Christ and God the Father. . . .

Yours sincerely,
A saved sinner
M. Nishizawa.

Sensei went at once and in turn to visit each of the families listed, and she took comfort to each of them. Mrs. Nishizawa thanked her most of all.

Only two days later an American officer called on Sensei. He had come to tell her that Nishizawa and one of the other converts had been executed the night before.

"They died triumphantly," he told her. "When the clock struck the midnight hour, the two men came out of the inner prison, their Testaments clasped in their manacled hands. They were singing, " 'Nearer, My God, to Thee,' and back in the cells the other prisoners sang: 'God Be With You Till We Meet Again.' "

"The two men knelt on the trap door, praying and offering praise to God," he went on. "Their faces were radiant."

Quickly Sensei bowed her head in prayer. The young officer waited until she was finished.

"I would like to accept Christ, too," he said. "I would like to meet my Maker as these men did." And so Sensei brought him, too, to the Savior.

Sensei was to hear from others of the war criminals before their executions. A Japanese poem came from a general: "The call for the execution is as sweet as the voice of the angels. Now I start on the journey to the Kingdom of God."

One of the last letters she received was from Hideyoshi Ishizaki, the third man to take a stand for Christ in the clemency interviews. Sensei could only brush back the tears as she read:

Teacher Smith:

I thank you very much for your guidance to lead me to Christ, especially to I who is a stranger to you.

Today I am going back to the Eternal life under the feet of God by His Grace. It is a joy which excels all. Brothers Nishizawa and Shibano have gone back to Him, and others, too, and now Brother Mizuguchi and I are going.

I am so grateful to God that I can go to Him in such peace and as a child of God. I owe it to your guidance and to Jesus Christ, and to my reading of the Bible. Under any circumstances the Almighty God saves those who are lost and those who are troubled.

I was afraid that I had to go on this journey alone with Brother Mizuguchi, but fortunately a Protestant chaplain, Captain O. W. Schoech, visited us this morning with a Bible and a hymnal. He read from the second chapter of Luke, from verse 25 to 35 together with us and encouraged us. We prayed that Christ would receive us as His servants by His Grace. I told the chaplain that I love verses 23 to 43 of the twenty-third chapter of Luke. The chaplain explained these verses to us. I told him that we wanted to sing some hymns which we had in our mind before we start this journey. He thought it was fine and asked us to give the hymnal to him when we were through with it. I consented to do so, and we picked up Nos. 507, 274, 306, 412, 441, and 563. We sang these hymns this morning from the bottom of our hearts until tears ran down. How happy we are! to go back to Him saved by His graceful hand. The chaplain visited us again in the afternoon to give us words of cheer; though I could not fully understand his English, I was consoled and encouraged. He told us he would accompany us to the last moment. I cannot thank too strongly for the great love of Christ . . . I pray that you would work harder for Jesus Christ, and also take great care of your body. May the mercy of Jesus Christ abide with you. Amen.

9 P.M. Feb. 11
Hideo Ishizaki

Sensei folded the letter and put it away with the others. She would keep them always, she knew, and in her heart she would always hold the memory of the men in Sugamo prison who went to Christ so triumphantly.

Epilogue

IT was what you might expect. Sensei was waiting for me when I arrived at Tokyo's Haneda Airport on a cool dark evening in November, 1964. The polite Japanese customs officials had waved me on and I made my way through the narrow aisle into the crowded waiting room. Sensei, dressed in a warm wool overcoat, beamed at me through her glasses and welcomed me to Japan. With her was Dr. Joe Gooden who had loyally accompanied her to the airport. His full beard made him look more like a professor than a missionary from Texas.

Soon we were wheeling along in a miniature taxi on the new throughway toward downtown Tokyo. The first building I recognized was the Kabuki Theater and just beyond was the neon glare of the Ginza—shopping center by day and Tokyo's Broadway by night.

"We're taking you to a smorgasbord dinner, thanks to Joe," Sensei announced. I smiled wanly, too tired to tell my warm-hearted hosts I was more interested in rest than in food. Smorgasbord in Tokyo? The Japanese can duplicate anything the rest of the world has to offer.

Sensei was wise enough to suggest that I get to bed early, so we headed for the Ochanomizu Christian Student Center in the university district a mile or so away. Sensei escorted me to a comfortable guest room in the building behind the center—the two-story structure that once had been the home of Asada San. I noticed that my bed was equipped with an American electric blanket which proved to be a godsend on chilly nights in a building without central heat. I soon fell asleep, too tired to examine my quarters.

Early next morning—Sensei usually gets up at five-thirty—she invited me to her combination dining room, kitchen, bedroom, and study—a tiny cubicle measuring eight by ten feet. This is Sensei's home—one room on the second floor of the house. Only the bare necessities are there: a single bed that looked as though it might have come from Ireland; a desk cluttered with papers; a little gas stove with a big blaze that provided heat for the room and also for the battered brass tea kettle that was singing a song of cheer.

An oak cupboard in one corner contained table linen, chinaware, and silverware. Sensei was setting a small table by a large bay window. On one side of the table was a comfortable chair for the guest and on the other a stool for the hostess.

"Sit over there in the chair and I'll give you some porridge. My mother always said porridge was like a poultice on your stomach. Then we'll have an egg and toast and tea . . . How do you like my little room? This is all I have and this is all I need."

I looked out the window. I realized I was looking out on Asada San's formal Japanese garden; even though it was November, it was still beautiful. A stone lantern was placed in a grove of evergreen trees through which wound white gravel walks. A few yellow chrysanthemums glowed against the dark greens.

Sensei talked as she continued with her breakfast chores. "When they moved the house I asked the carpenters to make that bay window for me so I could look out on the garden," she explained as she served the porridge. "I hope you don't mind condensed milk?"

The walls of Sensei's room were lined with pictures of those she cherished: a faded photograph of her regal-looking mother; the prim face of Adelaide Soal; the lovely vision of Kazue; formal portraits of Barclay Buxton and Paget Wilkes. A lithograph of Queen Elizabeth caught my eye.

Another window behind me looked out on the white stucco walls of the four-story student center—quite impersonal in the morning light. But later in the day laughing university students would be playing table tennis on the open deck at the second-story level.

After the breakfast things had been cleared away, Sensei took the photograph of Kazue from the wall. She removed her glasses to squint at the picture, holding it close to bring it into focus for her dimming sight. As she studied the likeness, Sensei seemed to absent herself from the room. With childlike intensity, she was reliving precious experiences of her eventful life. Her lips formed words that were not uttered.

"Dear Kazue," she murmured as she passed the photograph over to me. Then she resumed her animated conversation, discussing what our itinerary would be during my brief visit to Japan.

I soon could discern that Sensei, nearing eighty, was no recluse living in a cell. Her tiny chamber was the place from which she took off on her journeys. We had only begun our conversation when the telephone rang in the hall just outside her room.

"Muchi, muchi," she replied. Then a torrent of Japanese flowed from her lips, with the same ease that she had been speaking English to me. Her caller was Hanako, one of her Sunrise "girls" who had not spoken to her since Sensei returned from her trip to Great Britain and the United States.

Sensei came back into the room happy and stimulated by the phone conversation. We had not talked long before the phone rang again. Could she speak at Grant Heights? "Yes, of course, I'll be glad to come, but I'm busy this week and next because I have a visitor here from America."

Later in the morning she escorted me on a tour of the student center. She introduced me to three young men in the black uniforms of Chuo University. "These are Christian boys," she said. "I call them my bodyguard."

She rattled on in Japanese, willing to linger and visit with the young men. As she talked to the students, one could sense that she had established a pattern of self-giving that had become a natural and spontaneous part of her personality. She was inquiring of a young man about his brother and sister. One could feel her genuine concern from the tone of her voice.

The rest of the day was filled with interruptions. Some missionaries from the north of Japan announced they were coming to Tokyo to see a friend off on a plane to Canada. Sensei arranged for them to stay in a room that had been used for storage.

That evening she took me along with three women missionaries to a tempura dinner in a near-by student restaurant. We were the only Westerners in the place but Sensei was right at home.

In the days that followed we were traveling nearly every day. Even though she took my arm when we walked up and down the flights of stairs at the railroad stations, her zest for life was still strong. Now and then her faulty vision manifested itself, seeming to give her a sense of uncertainty when she was unable to locate familiar landmarks. But her enthusiasm was boundless.

"You ought to see the tuberculosis sanatorium the Kaji sisters operate at Ajiro," she told me. I had no idea how this would help me in writing her life story. Sensei had learned that three sisters of an aristocratic Japanese family were struggling to keep their little hospital for children going. Even though her own needs were great, she had introduced Dr. Bob Pierce of World Vision to the hospital work and encouraged him to give financial assistance. This was one of several Christian enterprises in which Sensei was currently interested. Even though there were critical needs at the student center, her heart seemed to embrace all Japan.

En route to Ajiro, we stopped at Atami, seacoast resort famed for its hot springs. Sensei took me to one of the spas so I could form my ideas first hand. A polite hotel manager insisted that we take a tour of the hotel. Sensei loved every minute of it.

As we traveled by bus from Atami to Ajiro, Sensei was eager for me to see the beauty of the rocky sea coast. I learned later that we could have gone by train direct to Ajiro, but she had planned a trip that I would enjoy.

As we talked to the Ajiro sisters about their hospital ministry, it became more than ever apparent that throughout her life, Sensei has always blended the words and the works of the gospel. Talking to people about Jesus Christ never has been separated from meeting need at the human level.

To Sensei, blankets for the victims of a typhoon or an earthquake, food for the hungry, toys for kindergarten children—all these fit into her concept of gospel effort. Her mission had a policy of engaging in evangelistic work exclusively, but Sensei thought in specific terms about the need of little girls. Yet Sunrise Home became a focus of evangelism not only for the little girls in her care but for the entire community of Akashi and surrounding villages. Since she lived the gospel, her words found ready acceptance.

That is how she still lives today. Like her Master, Sensei has been willing to be identified with publicans and sinners, to sit where they sit, to serve rather than to be served. Whether she is talking to a royal princess or a harlot, to an innocent child or a confused university student, a prisoner or a soldier, Sensei meets them with ease and self-assurance. I found that she was not dazzled by people of rank, yet she meets deprived people with grace. In each individual she finds the likeness and image of God.

Her story reminds one of the unfinished account of the Acts of the Apostles. She continues to perform exploits for the Lord. Like the disciples of the Early Church, she moves on with an inward sense of the Holy Spirit's direction and power. While there is a pilgrim aspect to her life, this is no purposeless wandering through a desert. Rather, she walks through life with a knowledge of God's immediate presence, One who directs her step by step and Who opens the way before her.

Yet Sensei, being a humble and a human person, recognizes that she has made many mistakes. She has experienced the bite of discipline, the joy of forgiveness. When you hear her laugh, you could never say she was "born religious."

But like her Lord she has not evaded the role of servant. Her life, to use a phrase from Oswald Chambers, has been "broken bread and poured-out wine."

Her Savior and Friend was once asked, "Lord, when saw we thee an hungered, and fed thee? or thirsty, and gave thee drink? When saw we thee a stranger, and took thee in? or naked, and clothed thee? Or when saw we thee sick, or in prison, and came unto thee?"

This has been a catalogue of Sensei's life. And it is as true today as when she first landed in Japan to work at Miss Penrod's rescue home for fallen women; or when she took in eighty-seven little strangers and fed and clothed them; or when she penetrated the fastness of Sugamo Prison to visit doomed men.

Sensei already knows the answer to the questions posed to our Lord: "Inasmuch as ye have done it unto one of the least of these my brethren, ye have done it unto me."

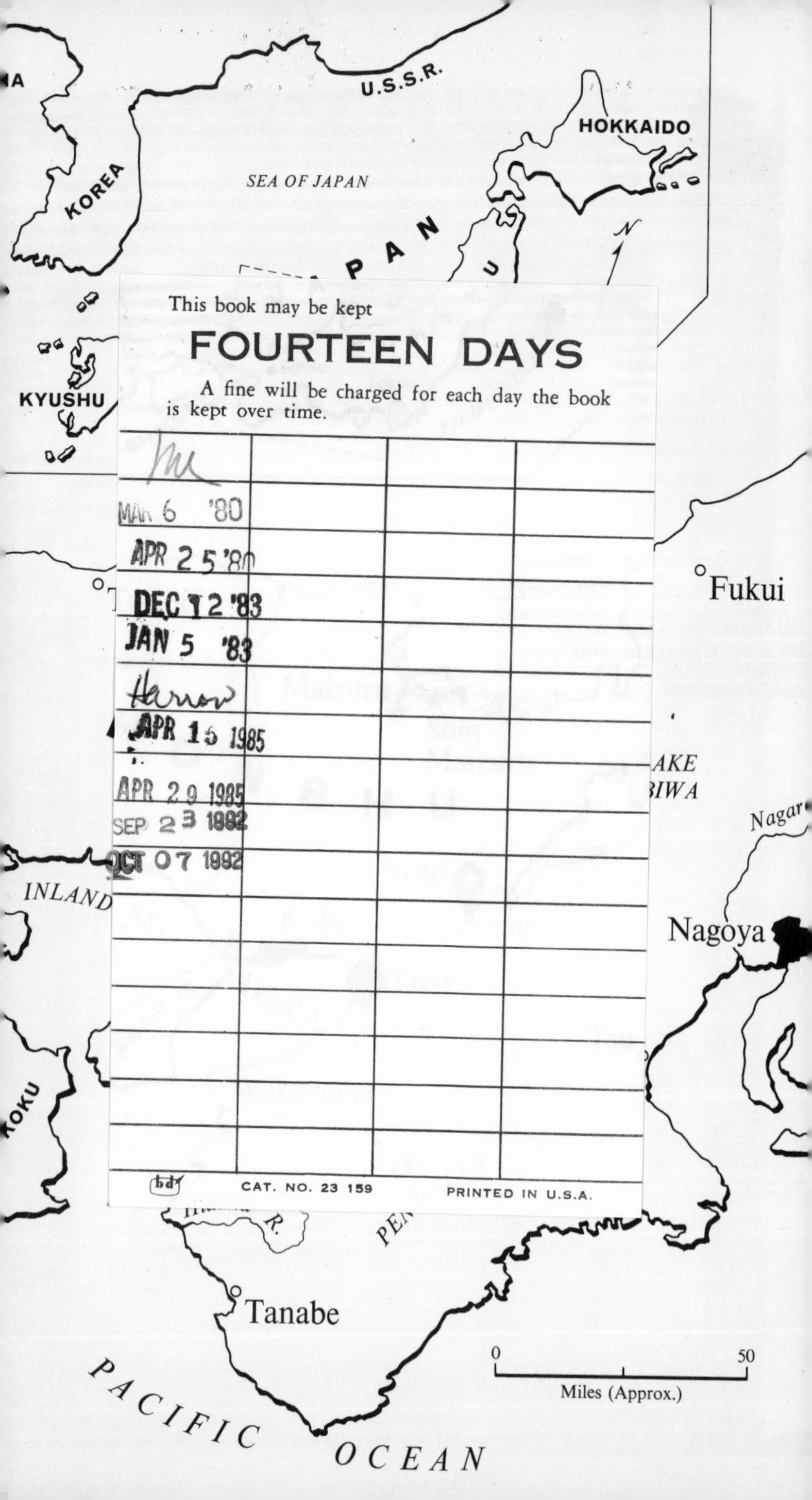
U.S.S.R.
HOKKAIDO
SEA OF JAPAN
KOREA
KYUSHU
Fukui
Nagoya
INLAND
Tanabe
PACIFIC
OCEAN
0
50
Miles (Approx.)